THE YAMI OF LAN-YU ISLAND

PORTRAIT OF A CULTURE IN TRANSITION

Douglas C. Smith

Published by
Phi Delta Kappa Educational Foundation
Bloomington, Indiana U.S.A.

Cover design by
Victoria Voelker

All photographs by
Douglas C. Smith

Library of Congress Catalog Card Number 98-68412
ISBN 0-87367-811-7
Copyright © 1998 by Douglas C. Smith
Bloomington, Indiana U.S.A.

DEDICATED TO

Dr. Bruce Clayton Flack, college president,
professor, scholar, sportsman, adventurer,
godfather, and father par excellence,
and a dear friend.

ACKNOWLEDGMENTS

Field-based research on Lan-yu Island formed the foundation for this essay on the Yami people. During that research I was able to take hundreds of photographs, to interview a number of Chinese scholars from Taiwan, to talk with Yami individuals of all ages and circumstances, and to live with the Yami in order to develop a fuller sense of their culture, their fears, and their strengths. I am particularly indebted to Professor Wu Che-gung, who took me under his wing and guided me on my quest to understand the Yami. Also assisting me with this effort were Michael P. Riccards, Rebecca Drawbaugh, Cathay Yvette-Nikka Smith, Grace L. Henderson, Suzannah Yu-Fong-Lo Smith, Heather McNaught, and Donovan R. Walling.

TABLE OF CONTENTS

INTRODUCTION

The Yami of Lan-yu Island are a small group of Asian aborigines whose homeland lies about 60 miles southeast of Taiwan and is governed by the Chinese government in Taipei.

Once, not really so long ago, living on a self-contained island could ensure to a people a certain continuity of native culture, a certain "purity." Modern times have destroyed this idyll. And so the Yami culture is now rapidly changing. No longer strictly aboriginal, the Yami are making "progress," according to the standards of the developed world.

On several occasions I have had the opportunity to live with the Yami, to converse with them, to ask questions, and to observe the behaviors that define this island people. Out of these experiences as a participant-observer, I have collected my impressions of Yami culture, society, and education in this informal study.

"Informal" is a key word. This study is intended as an introduction for interested readers who may, or may not, be familiar with cultural anthropology. My intent is to draw a portrait of a culture in transition and, in so doing, to raise questions about what that transition might mean in the context of how Western educators, in particular, address cultural issues.

This study necessarily touches on many macroenvironmental issues, such as geography, rituals, education and intelligence, child rearing and teaching, food production and distribution, shamanism, boat building, marriage, ghosts, and more. However, the main lesson to be drawn is not in the particulars but in the transitions that are being forced by the encroachment of "civilization." And that raises a larger issue, one often neglected in teaching about cultures and societies: What is the nature of civilization? And what makes a civilization civilized?

Chapter
One

ADRIFT IN
THE PACIFIC BASIN

From the moon the earth appears to be a blue and green ball. Blue dominates: water. And of these blue expanses the greatest is the Pacific Basin. It stretches from the Arctic Circle to the Antarctic ice pack and from the west coast of the Americas to the jagged east coast of Asia. The sheer size of the Pacific Basin is difficult to comprehend. From the Arctic Circle to Antarctica is approximately 10,000 miles. The largest distance from east to west is said to be between Singapore and Panama, some 12,350 miles.

But this vast area is anything but empty water. In fact, it is littered with thousands of islands, islets, and atolls. More than 25,000 land masses are estimated to dot this vast ocean, many in the region known as Oceania. Most are uninhabited. Some are mere outcroppings of coral that surface only during the periods when the moon's pull causes tidal fluctuations of the mighty Pacific. Others are large: Japan, Australia, New Zealand, Taiwan, the Philippine Islands.

Each island in has its own geological history, but the land masses can be classified in four major categories. Coral formations are one. Islands formed in this way generally have a low profile, though they often are large in area. Among the many islands in the Pacific Basin, the coral atolls tend to be the least hospitable to flora and human and animal habitation.

3

A second method by which some islands of the South Pacific came into existence is volcanic eruption. Hawaii best represents this type of geologic history. A characteristic of this type of island is one or more cone-shaped mountains that thousands of years ago were volcanoes that erupted beneath the sea and built upon themselves to create a land mass. The land beneath the mountain peaks weathered over time. Wind and sea leveled much of the land surrounding the cone, and thus the islands could be inhabited by the South Pacific boat people as they followed the various currents from Asia and possibly from the west coast of the Americas, as Thor Heyerdahl suggested after his successful Galapagos Islands expedition of 1953 (Heyerdahl 1963). Important support for the South American contact thesis is the widespread use of the South American sweet potato in Polynesia before European contact. Some islands, of course, such as the big island of Hawaii itself, still feature active volcanoes.

A third method is referred to as "high island" or "continental island" formation. New Guinea is a good example of a continental island. These few land masses are large and tend to have ecological and geological characteristics that are similar to those of the continents to which they are nearest, though on a smaller scale. Complete ecosystems of mountains, rivers, swamps, hills, deserts, deltas, numerous fauna and flora types, harbors, and regional weather patterns within the confines of the island are characteristics of the high/continental model. Vili Levu, the largest of the Fiji Islands, is another example of a continental island.

Finally, a fourth method is illustrated by the "break-away" islands. Some of the larger islands are break-away portions of a nearby land mass. Taiwan, formerly Formosa Island, many thousands of years ago was attached to the southeastern coast of China. Shifts in the earth's crust caused the land to rise and fall. The area between Taiwan and the Asian mainland fell and formed the Formosa Strait. This last method is pertinent because a similar geological condition occurred with Lan-yu, probably about the same time that the island of Taiwan split from the east coast of what is now Fukien Province in mainland China. The terrain of Lan-yu Island, once known as Botel Tobaga, and the rocks and flora found there indicate the previous connection with what is now the bustling island of Taiwan some 60 miles away.

Every type of weather is found in the Pacific, and each island group has its own ecological and meteorological environment. Therefore, generalizations become impossible. Similarly, this vast region is populated by peoples who, like the islands on which they live, differ markedly from one another.

To characterize the people of Lan-yu Island — the Yami — it is first necessary to survey the general area in which they reside. The Pacific is a turbulent region characterized by storms, volcanoes, earthquakes, tsunamis, wild currents, hidden coral reefs, and, on the various islands, diseases unknown to those living in more northern or southern latitudes. These islands — among them Polynesia, the Mariannas, Micronesia, and Melanesia — often are considered among the most aesthetically pleasing locales, but the people who live there have had to endure great hardships. Thus the various island cultures have evolved to address their singular enviroments.

Many scholars have attempted to trace the origins of the inhabitants of the various Pacific islands. But definitive answers are hard to come by, as there is little agreement among ethnologists, geographers, linguists, social historians, geneticists, and serologists. While the ethnological ingredients that make up the polytypic population of the island peoples is still debated, it does appear that groups wandered out of Asia, perhaps from as far north as Mongolia, and populated the islands of the region.

This leads one to conclude that a mixing of peoples from all over Asia (from northern China down the Asian coast and across even to Australia) characterized the migration. Whether the exodus was a few separate, major migrations or simply a gradual egress of small groups is not known. Birdsell (1949) does suggest, however, that there is no evidence (as has been suggested by other anthropologists) of sub-Saharan African elements in the island regions of the South Pacific, even though many dark-complexioned peoples live there.

In all but a few cases (for example, Pitcairn Island) records do not exist to explain how a given island was populated. And legends, folklore, cultural and physiological attributes, and linguistic patterns are not able to give definitive answers related to origins. The mixing of blood has made the subject of provenance problematic. In short, the Pacific population today is the product of "generations of racial churning, in which the evolutionary processes of mutation, migration, natural selection, genetic drift, and selective mating have effectively contributed to the racial diversity so demonstrated there today" (Swindler 1962, p. 41).

Geological and ecological tensions created the lands in the Pacific Basin, and such forces continue to redefine the biogeography of this region. Conflict and struggle also characterize the evolutionary process of humankind and the efforts of men and women to endure the challenges imposed on them, particularly the inhabitants of the Pacific's many islands. James A. Michener, novelist, cultural critic, historian, and world adventurer, sums up the grandeur of creativity in these words from his one of his most famous novels, *Hawaii*:

> Millions upon millions of years ago, when the continents were already formed and the principal features of the earth had been decided, there existed, then as now, one aspect of the world that dwarfed all others. It was a mighty ocean, resting uneasily to the east of the largest continent, a restless ever-changing, gigantic body of water that would later be described as pacific.
>
> Over its brooding surface immense winds swept back and forth, whipping the waters into towering waves that crashed down upon the world's seacoasts, tearing away rocks and eroding the land. . . .
>
> Agitated by a moon stronger than now, immense tides ripped across the tremendous ocean, keeping it in a state of torment.
>
> Scores of millions of years before man had risen from the shores of the ocean to perceive its grandeur and to venture forth upon its turbulent waves, this eternal sea existed, larger than any other of the earth's features, vaster than the sis-

ter oceans combined, wild, terrifying in its immensity and imperative in its universal role.

I have used this chapter to set the scene for my study and Michener's elegant prose to conjure up an image, or rather a set of images, against which to paint the portrait of a people, the Yami. My intent in this brief treatment is to write for American educators, in particular, and to introduce readers to an aboriginal culture that is, if you will, "cloistered" by nature and seemingly at odds with the modern world. And yet the Yami and those of us who people the "civilized" world have much in common, especially when technology and the other trappings of modern life are stripped away. Societies develop in response to their needs: to survive a hostile environment, to be fed, to produce generations. In spite of superficial differences, the needs of one people are the needs of all. The shared qualities of human existence remain. This is an important lesson, and it leads to other lessons, not about how to change the modern American family or education or social life, but about the passages humans travel to individual and collective fulfillment.

Any description of a people and their way of life is subjective, especially when one has lived in their midst only briefly. As a consequence, all cross-cultural analyses are at best partial stories and unfinished studies. This is certainly true of my exposure to the Yami people. And the Yami culture is as complex as any other. One peels an onion; a culture is revealed in layer upon layer. At the same time, I am conscious that doing fieldwork is contradictory by nature. The goal is to learn as much as possible about an unfamiliar society — certainly a necessarily intrusive endeavor — and at the same time to leave unblemished, unaffected, the society under scrutiny.

Chapter
Two

FIRST CONTACT

There are places on Earth that are destined by their history, their location, and their beauty to stir the emotions. Shrouded in mystery and blessed with centuries of splendid isolation, these places bring delight to the visitor. Essentially different from other places where one travels, these locations are rare. To the traveler far from home, they become sanctuaries of the past, special and therefore wonderful. The small island of Lan-yu off the southeast coast of Taiwan is such a place.

I was first invited to visit Lan-yu and to do field-based research on the culture of the Yami aboriginal people on this small islet while I was a visiting professor at Tunghai University in Taiwan. After that initial visit, I returned to Lan-yu on other occasions, having become fascinated by the land and its inhabitants. The comparatively unstudied Yami (at least by Western scholars) appealed to me for a variety of reasons, the most significant being that I had been allowed to become a participant-observer in their society. By this I mean that I had been allowed to live and interact with the Yami as a fellow human and, at the same time, I had been able to step back and to observe them as a scholar. These encounters with the Yami led to more study and, eventually, to the development of this book.

At this point I should interject a few words about my philosophy of cultural anthropology. My thinking about the Yami and about comparative cultural analysis in general has been shaped by much reading. I would particularly recommend to students of cultural comparison such works as Ruth Benedict's *Patterns of Culture*, Colin M. Turnbull's *The Mountain People*, and almost any of the anthropological accounts written by the indomitable Margaret Mead. But perhaps the main influence on my notions about aboriginal life can be traced to one book, *The Mind of Primitive Man* (1911), written by Franz Boas. It was Boas who revolutionized the study of anthropology and cultural psychology. Prior to his writing, scholars believed that culture was a fixed entity in which all societies participated to one extent or another. Culture was evolutionary: Folk with primitive technology were at an early stage; those with technological know-how had reached a more advanced stage and were, in fact, more "civilized."

Franz Boas' main achievement was to redefine the meaning of "primitive." He believed that anthropologists needed to study the differences between cultures and the ways in which various societies evolved in response to their environment and external influences. Prior to Boas, it was widely believed that aboriginal peoples were merely "backward," not culturally distinct. Technological advance, thus a form of "civilization," was seen as evidence of cultural "progress." But Boas set in place a new notion, which said that the circumstances experienced by a people — environment, geography, and so on — determined a society's destiny, rather than race, language, or other factors. Therefore "civilization" was not a continuum along which "progress" might be made. Cultures were distinct. Both Benedict and Mead became disciples of Boas, whose view now dominates scholarship in cultural anthropology.

The aboriginal peoples of Taiwan and the nearby islands usually are identified as eight distinct tribes, or groups: Ami, Atayal, Botan, Lukai, Paiwan, Peinan, Ping pu, and Yami. Each group has its own culture, mores, rituals, and geographic area. Only the Yami may be termed *islet people*; all of the others are farming and mountain-dwelling folk.

Most early accounts of these aboriginal peoples present an unrealistically harsh view. A remarkable account of Asian life was written by the Reverend George Leslie Mackay, who devoted 23 years to helping the Taiwanese. His book, *From Far Formosa* (1895) is in many respects an excellent account of life on the island. But Mackay's humanitarian values did not, it would seem, extend to the aborigines: "The longer my experience among [the natives] the plainer appears to me the inferiority of the Malayan. For downright cruelty and cutthroat baseness the aborigines far outdistance the Chinese." Mackay devotes an entire chapter to headhunting as it was carried out by the native peoples against the Chinese. But in fairness it should be noted that both the "civilized" Chinese and the aborigines committed heinous, genocidal actions during their ongoing conflagrations. Perhaps more noteworthy, but omitted by Mackay, is the fact that the only indigenous tribe that never practiced headhunting was the Yami of Lan-yu.

Just as there were tensions between white settlers and Native Americans in the New World, so were there tense relationships between the ruling Chinese and their indigenous populations. Early Chinese contacts with native peoples were marked by an attitude of "invade and conquer." Native groups were subjugated or removed from their land and the land confiscated.

In more recent memory the Japanese occupation and control of the Taiwan region from 1895 until 1945 brought some relief from the Chinese attitude of oppression after literally hundreds of years of frontier bedlam. The Japanese saw the aboriginal tribes as distinct — though perhaps related to the Japanese themselves through some distant ancestry — but, moreover, capable of "progress." Yasoburo Takekoshi, a leading scholar at the turn of the century, wrote:

> In 1903, the employees of Mr. Dogura took several savage girls to the Domestic Exhibition which was held in Osaka. Their few months stay in Japan thoroughly Japanised them, so much so, indeed, that by the end of the time, they looked at first glance almost like Osaka girls, especially as

they all had their hair done up just like Japanese. This instance was often referred to at that time as a convincing proof of the feasibility of civilizing and training the savages. (1907, p. 229)

It also was Takekoshi who suggested: "I entertain a firm conviction that our Japanese ancestors and these aboriginal savages are in some way blood relations" (p. 218).

Today more than 250,000 aboriginal people reside as citizens in Taiwan, but their lives are hard. They are less prosperous and less healthy than the Chinese inhabitants of the island.

Although this number includes the Yami on Lan-yu Island, they are largely overlooked. Indeed, the disparaging comments made about aborigines throughout history have been directed toward those living on Taiwan itself. Little direct contact has ever existed between the big island and little Lan-yu. And so, while the Yami occasionally were raided by Chinese or Western marauders, they were spared many of the hardships that befell other tribes.

This isolation, which I have referred to previously as "splendid isolation," was splendid because it allowed the Yami to retain a unique culture that was essentially unaltered until very recently. Not only was the evolutionary process — "progress" — slowed by this isolation, but also any cross-cultural "adulteration" of the Yami was considerably diminished.

Lan-yu (also seen as Lan Yü) lies in the Pacific along the 22nd Parallel in a direct line east of Taiwan's southernmost city, Hengch'un. The island has been inhabited for perhaps 10,000 years. Whatever the original gene pool of the Yami, over the years it has been only minimally "adulterated" by travelers who have chosen to remain on the island and by visitors from China, Japan, and the West. And this is true even though the population of Lan-yu is small. The population of the Yami in 1939 numbered 1,777. By 1964 that figure had grown to about 2,000; and by 1996 the population numbered some 2,700 living in the island's several villages.

Although Lan-yu is a break-away island from the larger land mass of Taiwan, the Yami are unlike their aboriginal counterparts there. The Yami are the only native people who do not live in mountainous areas, instead relying on fishing as a major source of food. The Yami also present a contrast to the people of Yap, a small group of islands about 1,450 miles southeast of Lan-yu. The Yap people have many customs that are similar to those of the Yami. And, like the Yami, they are a "boat culture." But the Yap people are physically and linguistically unlike the Yami. On the other hand, the inhabitants of islets in the northern Philippine region (particularly Batan and Babuyan Islands) are similar in appearance and language to the Yami, but their ways of life differ.

In short, the origins of the Yami of Lan-yu are unknown. Different theories abound as to whether their ancestors came from China or from the Malay-Borneo area. It is probable that the Yami have their provenance in the islands of the Malay Archipelago. When asked where their forefathers came from, they always mention a southerly direction.

Another explanation might be that the ancient Yami hail from one of the Philippine Islands. The language of the Yami is much more similar to the dialects spoken on the northern Philippine island than it is to the linguistic patterns found among the aboriginal people in either Taiwan, Vietnam, or the coastal region of mainland China. This similarity, of course, suggests that the first Yami might have traveled to Lan-yu from Batan or Malaysia, a strong possibility considering the natural directions of the ocean currents. The Pacific currents that sweep past Lan-yu first touch Thailand, Malaysia, Java, Sumatra, Borneo, and up to the Taiwan Strait. Some tend to veer to the eastern coast of Taiwan and thence bathe Orchid Island. A return to Batan from Lan-yu would have been virtually impossible, because to do so would have required the Yami to paddle their canoes against a major south-north current.

**Chapter
Three**

ORCHID ISLAND

"Lan-yu" can best be translated as Island of the Orchid Flower, a name appropriate to this idyllic islet. It resembles, on a small scale, the topography of Taiwan proper. But the similarity ends with the topography.

Until 1945 the island of Lan-yu often was called Hung-tou-yu, or Redhead Island, probably because a vitamin deficiency tends to color the islanders' hair. After 1945, when Taiwan was ceded from Japan back to China, the island was named Lan-yu, or Orchid Island. However, most older maps and much of the academic literature that deals with the region refers to Lan-yu as Botel Tobago, which also was its name during the Japanese occupation from 1895 to 1945. (Lan-yu also will be seen on modern maps as Lan Yü.)

Four of us made the first trip in which I participated: three Chinese scholars — a sociologist, a hydraulic engineer, and a law professor — and me, a historian and educator. Our "adventure" was sponsored by Taiwan's department of education, and our activities were coordinated by the local Chinese school recently built on Lan-yu.

At 60 miles off the southeast coast of Taiwan, Lan-yu is a subtropical island with an average annual temperature of 26°C (79°F). January is the coldest month, and July and August are the hot ones. This makes Lan-yu somewhat hotter than Taiwan, which actually straddles the tropical and subtropical zones. And, indeed, the vegetation of Lan-yu is more akin to that found on the more southerly Philippine islands, particularly Batan, than to the flora of Taiwan itself.

In some respects Lan-yu might be considered the furthest northern outpost of the Polynesian islands. Its shape is said to resemble a clenched fist, and its extent is a mere 17.5 square miles. Although Taiwan is its nearest large neighbor, there are other, smaller islands that are closer. Green Island, another spot of isolation and beauty, is 35 miles north of Lan-yu. Little Orchid Island, or Little Lan-yu, as it is called, is a large rock formation — really an atoll — about 4 miles south of Lan-yu. The next large island is Batan, which lies to the south about 90 miles away.

(Little Orchid Island, incidentally, is popular among some inhabitants for fishing and collecting coral and shells. But mostly the Yami see the atoll as dangerous because of the currents and winds. And ghosts are said to reside there.)

Lan-yu is a volcanic island, though the last eruption was many thousands of years ago; and volcanic formation was probably not the island's main history. But the island soil tends to be stony as a result. Farm land is at a premium, and great care is taken to ensure that three different crops can be harvested annually in most locations. Clans, rather than individuals, hold this valuable farm property.

The 17.5 square miles of Lan-yu make an island that, at its widest, is about 11 miles across. Its circumference is some 32 miles, and the only paved road on the island follows the coast. A complete circuit by car can be made in two hours. Much of that circuit is marked by beaches that are lovely to look at against the bright blue ocean but treacherous under foot, because they are composed of sharp stones, shell fragments, and coral dust. Swimming, at least for the uninitiated, can be difficult.

But I move too quickly. The island merits a fuller description, because, in fact, Lan-yu combines four physical environments. The first is the ocean itself, vast and blue, similar to what can be seen by a visitor to Hawaii or even the Caribbean. The Yami are a "boat culture," which I will explain later; but this makes the ocean doubly valued. It possesses a spiritual component that far outweighs its practical value.

The second is the shore, a combination of stony beaches punctuated along the island's circumference by strangely shaped coral and volcanic rocks, many of great size, that sit at the water's edge. The coral and rock formations — some as tall as a 12-story building — were born of erosion by the wind and water, and they are both beautiful and strange. At dusk, in particular, these fantastic natural formations can become frightening in aspect, as the sun draws eerie shadows in the crevasses and holes that animate them. Much of the Yami's fear of ghosts and demons, of which I will write more later, can be felt when walking among these giants that seem to take on the shapes of demons, human figures, ships, birds, and mystical cities.

The beaches are composed of jagged coral and shells and sharp, white rocks. They vary in width from only a few yards to more than a hundred from water's edge to grassy land. In a few places the mountains come down directly to the water, and there is no beach at all. But where there are beaches, they play an important role in Yami life. Many inhabitants follow a daily ritual of coming to the beach each morning to bathe, and the proximity of the beaches obviates the standard necessities of "civilized" life: toilets, plumbing, outhouses, and the like. The ocean serves as a communal bath in every aspect. My own experience suggests that the Yami, young and old alike, maintain a natural cleanliness and universal good hygiene. The foul smells that can be found in most primitive villages, such as the aboriginal enclaves of Taiwan, are not evident on Lan-yu.

The beaches also are a place of community in another way. Fragrances drift across them from the seaside villages: flowers, smoke from cooking fires, sun-drying fish, roasting yams and taro roots. Children seem to spend most of their time on the beaches, playing in the shallow water and running wild and naked in groups in the splashing surf. In spite of the sharp stones, Yami

17

children and adults feel no need for shoes (though I found them a necessity).

I stated previously that the Yami are a "boat culture." Thus within easy reach along the flat stony stretches, elaborately decorated, ocean-going canoes rest, waiting for the active fishing season from March to August. These beautiful craft serve symbolic and spiritual, as well as practical, purposes, which I will discuss in another chapter.

Children's laughter and chatter compete with another sound. The surf crashing on the beach is a regular part of the Yami's life. It is a relaxing sound when the winds are gentle and the sea is calm. But during the typhoon season in the fall the sound of the ocean pounding the rock formations and the beach is loud and invasive. This rhythmic noise is like the sound of a huge, beating heart and suggests to the Yami that their land is alive. Again, it is easy to understand why superstition and shamanism are part of the lifeforce of these people. They are a quiet, gentle folk; but all about them the forces of nature dominate their tiny island. Controlling their own destiny is constantly challenged by these forces.

A third environment lies inland, where the island stretches out as grassy, fertile plains. In most areas this flatland forms a zone between the seashore and the mountains. Were it not for this land, Lan-yu probably would be just another uninhabited atoll in the vast Pacific. This level rim of fields and grasslands forms a mini-plateau that offers sufficient space for crops to be grown, game to be hunted, and villages to be built. Although it extends from only a few hundred feet to more than a mile in width, the flatland is sufficient to give protection from the sea during turbulent times. It is literally a "circle of peace," complete with running fresh water from the central mountains.

Work that is not boat-related is accomplished in this circle, along with family activities and relaxation. Trees provide shade and lumber, and in the trees many varieties of birds can be heard singing day and night. The Yami live in six villages dotted in this circle, and the villages are connected by paths and rough roads.

A more recent, "civilized" road, constructed in the 1960s, now rings the island, cutting through the plateau. It joins all of the villages and has facilitated a small amount of tourism.

The fourth environment is the mountains, which seem to be astonishingly high for such a comparatively small land mass. They form the nine-nobbed spine of Lan-yu, in places reaching peaks 546 meters from sea level. These mountains are covered with tropical vegetation and mountain grasses. Streams and rivers vein these volcanic remnants, which now are smooth and rich in soil. Here, the Yami hunt small animals and birds, gather wild fruit, and collect wood for their boats, homes, and handicrafts. In past troubled times, the mountain woodlands also provided refuge; but these days they are more simply a peaceful retreat. Mountain streams supply fresh water, and rivers run swiftly, often cascading in waterfalls. Some of the waterfalls empty directly — and spectacularly — into the sea. The largest waterfall plunges more than 200 meters and produces a noise that can be heard at a good distance. Its mist forms a small cloud that, on still days, hangs motionless and ethereal.

While mountain fresh water and salty ocean water are plentiful, water storage is a problem. The amount of rainfall determines how big the problem will be. Crop irrigation depends on the streams from the mountains, which, in turn, depend on plentiful rains. A dry year can wreak havoc on the food supply. Fortunately, droughts are rare on Lan-yu, and rainfall is regular. Winter and spring are the rainy seasons, and rain water is stored in large barrels near the Yami homes against the dry seasons.

Only one route winds its way to the top of the mountain range, Redhead Mountain, the highest location on the island at slightly more than 546 meters above sea level. From this lofty peak one can see the true beauty of the island and the blue ocean that surrounds it. On a very clear day one can just make out the mainland of Taiwan; it seems to shimmer in the distance through the sun and vapor from the Pacific. Green Island, the small atoll about 35 miles to the north, also can be seen in this tentative way.

The interior mountains of Lan-yu boast tropical vegetation, rivers and streams of fresh water, and several spectacular waterfalls, the largest plunging more than 200 meters.

My first encounter with Redhead Mountain was on that first trip to Lan-yu, when my three Chinese colleagues and I decided to make the trek to the summit. Although the actual distance is not great, the hot sun, a steep path, and high humidity made the hike a demanding ordeal. The rough, one-lane road to the top zigzags madly, and frequent stops were necessary to avoid heat exhaustion. Once we reached the peak, we were able to stop at a small, government-operated weather and communications station. A Taiwanese family maintains this Spartan facility year-round.

Before I close this chapter of first impressions, I want to comment on Lan-yu's creatures — or, rather, their absence. Relatively few animals and birds live on the island. One reason, of course, is the vast expanse of Pacific Ocean, which makes migration difficult. But another reason is that the Yami have hunted the animals and birds nearly to extinction. Migrating birds, in particular, appear to sense instinctively that Lan-yu is to be avoided, because Yami children seem to like nothing better than "bird-on-a-stick" roasted over a charcoal fire.

The scarcity of animals and birds is matched by a similar dearth of insects, which was a pleasant surprise. The constant winds and overall good hygiene on the island seem to account for this fact. Mosquitoes and the diseases they often carry do not exist on Lan-yu, in contrast to the situation in the southern half of Taiwan, where mosquitoes are a problem.

Geography and the human condition always have been closely related. Modern technology has superseded this relationship in some ways. Difficult distances are spanned with the ease of machinery. Heating and air conditioning alter the climate to suit our needs. But where technology has not advanced, as on Lan-yu, the close relationship between place and people is maintained.

This notion strikes home while sitting on one of the eastern beaches. Here, in the morning, the red-gold sun rises out of the Pacific. The birds that remain on Lan-yu strike up tunes in the fields and in the mountain forests. Children laugh along the jagged shore, and the smells of village life waft on the ever-present breeze. By late afternoon the sun has slipped behind the high peaks, and shadows have begun to play among the fantastic rock formations on the shore. The moon rises and stars appear.

On the leeward side of Lan-yu the sun crests the mountains later and lingers longer. The three villages there get to watch it sink into the ocean at day's end. Only one village, Langtau, situated at the northern tip of the island, enjoys the best of both worlds. Its sun both rises and sets in the Pacific, which is perhaps an apt metaphor for the fate of Lan-yu itself.

For centuries the Pacific kept Lan-yu as its own, and the Yami enjoyed their "splendid isolation." Today the great ocean also is bringing those who gradually are changing Lan-yu. Some changes are for good: modern medicine and health care, better housing, and education. But paradise enhanced also can mean paradise corrupted. While the Chinese government of Taiwan undoubtedly can improve some aspects of Yami life, the "official" influence and the influx of tourists also are altering Yami culture and society. Like the island breezes, these influences are constant, and they are reshaping the Yami just as the everpresent Lan-yu winds have reshaped the volcanic monoliths along the shore.

INTO THE VILLAGES

The Yami live in six villages dotted around the island. The villages tend to sit adjacent to small bays, which make it easier to launch canoes and provide some protection for the children who dash along the beaches and play in the surf, where they also chase fish and sand crabs.

The villages, set back from the beaches on the flat grassland, are characterized by stone walls that are erected not so much to mark property lines or to offer privacy but to serve as windbreaks. (Similar walls can be seen on the Korean island of Cheju.) Vegetable plots will be found behind these walls; and when the winds blow, that is where old men will sit smoking cigarettes and children will play. The walls are most necessary during the fall, when the winds become especially strong.

Fresh water for drinking, cooking, and a small amount of irrigation comes from mountain streams. Women carry the water in large buckets to their homes and gardens. There is no distribution system or pipes to carry the water to the villages, much less to individual dwellings.

Village layouts are chaotic. No central structure, such as a temple or municipal building, dominates. Within the village wall, houses, individual walled gardens, trees, and other features are scattered haphazardly. "Streets" form a maze to the uninitiated visitor, who also must be alert to other hazards, including low ceilings, ditches, open basement doorways, protruding platforms, and small children scampering about.

While the apparent chaos of a village dominates one's first impressions — and all six villages are similar — there is a hidden sophistication at work. Each village is populated by a different clan. Within the village each family maintains three different houses. This is a unique feature of Yami life. Neither the other aboriginal groups of Taiwan nor the Polynesian islanders adhere to this standard. Which of the three houses is used at any given time is determined by the season (or the weather) and certain events. The houses consist of a main house (or "winter house"), a "social house," and a summer house.

The main house is the most elaborate of the three. It also requires the greatest engineering skill to construct. Built below ground level, the main house is warm in the harsh and windy winter months and cool during the very hot summer months, when a kind of heat paralysis seems to set in about midday for several weeks. To create the main house, workers dig a large hole that they then face with stone, rather like a crude basement. Stone walls rise out of the ground several feet. The earthen floor, some five to seven feet below ground level, is tamped and covered with boards. Above this chamber a circular, slanted roof is raised using wooden beams that support layers of dry grass. The grass is woven over and around the beams to ensure a waterproof covering.

Because the winters on Lan-yu are very wet, drainage is extremely important. The main house is protected from moisture by an ingeneous system. Rainwater flows from the slanted roof, down the front stone wall to a stone patio and into a specially designed rock drainage ditch that leads it away from the sunken living space. If the area around a house should become flooded during a particularly nasty monsoon, then the inhabitants can leave the house by means of specially mounted boards on the roof, which lead to a stone wall and, eventually, to dry ground.

The main house usually has two or three windows that can be closed with shutters that control the flow of air and sunlight. The roof features a smoke hole that can be opened or closed as needed. Typically the Yami endure copious amounts of smoke and heat, which are allowed to remain in the house but seem to be of little concern to the inhabitants. But most of the cooking is done outside. Only when the weather is very cold and windy do the Yami use their indoor wood stoves for cooking.

Decorations in the main house are of two types. Beautiful and elaborate carvings decorate all of the exposed wooden beams and support pillars. These carvings are similar in design to the decorations that can be seen on the Yami canoes. The other type of decoration consists of goat horns. Hung from the ceiling, the goat horns are seen as trophies and a sign of the family's social status. In some houses goat horns literally cover the ceiling, representing many generations of the family that has lived there. I should perhaps mention that the Yami tend to be rather short in stature. When I visited their homes, I found myself constantly ducking to avoid bumping door frames and goat horns. But in other respects these below-ground dwellings seem rather spacious, in part because belongings are neatly stowed and the houses are kept clean.

The second type of house is the "social house." Situated near the main house, this structure more closely resembles most Westerners' idea of a house. The social house is about 20' x 20' with a wood-beam, thatched roof, which sometimes rises as much as seven feet above a wooden floor. The walls are wood and, like the beams and pillars of the main house, elaborately decorated with carvings.

As when I visited several main houses, I was impressed with how clean and well-organized these buildings were in all of the villages on Lan-yu. Messy work — cleaning fish, butchering game, preparing food — invariably is done outdoors. I observed neither unpleasant odors nor insects in these work houses. Children ran freely through buildings; old people sat in the doorways; and men worked on wood projects in these houses, usually using the floor as their work station.

A favorite pastime of Yami men is carving small dolls for the children of the village. These figures usually are made of clay but

The Yami main home is constructed to protect its inhabitants from the elements. The below-ground dwelling stays warm in winter and cool in summer.

When it rains, as it often does during the winter months, the Yami main house is constructed to drain away the water by means of a stone-lined drainage ditch, which can be seen in this photograph.

The "social house" or "work house" of the Yami is designed for labor, commerce, and communication. Outside the social house in this photo, work has stopped temporarily on a small canoe, next to which can be seen a pile of wood shavings.

The Yami summer house, or "deck house," stands tall to catch the island breezes. Men often spend the afternoon smoking and napping in their summer houses.

sometimes are carved from native woods. The subjects include people, pigs, goats, chickens, fish, and, not surprisingly, boats. Most of these dolls are simple in form and easily remind one of trinkets made by other Pacific islanders, such as the peoples of Samoa, Yap, or Fiji. But the boats are a different matter; they are finely carved with elaborate detail.

The social house also is referred to as the "work house," and, indeed, it is a multipurpose structure. The Yami conduct all their business in these structures. The social house is used for commerce (often trading fish for vegetables and vice versa), as a family factory for making everything from canoe paddles to clothing and jewelry, as a workplace for repairing fishing nets, and, of course, as a place for socializing with friends and neighbors. When guests visit, food and drink are served to them in the social house. Chairs and tables are few; most people sit on the hard wooden floor to smoke, eat, and discuss their adventures and problems. The Yami love to talk, and the social house is the site for long evenings of discussion, particularly when guests from another village come calling.

For cooking and eating, the Yami use ceramic pots, which they also make in the social house; however, the pots are fired on the beach. Pots are formed as cooking pans, water jars, bowls, plates, and drinking glasses. Firing, which turns the finished pot a brick-red color, is normally done on a sunny day in an area of the beach that has been "cleansed" of evil influences. The pots are set among hot coals for several hours to ensure their integrity. Pot-making requires great skill, and those members of the community who acquire this craft are held second in esteem only to boat builders.

The grass roof, solid walls, and wooden floor of the social house work well to keep out both soft rains and hot sun most of the time, but the strong winds and intense heat of mid-summer drive the Yami either to the sturdier main house or to the cooler summer house.

The third type of Yami dwelling is the summer house, or "deck house." This structure is really a roofed deck on stilts. Where the main house offers cool comfort in bad weather, the summer house offers night breezes that relieve the oppressive humid heat of mid-summer in the Pacific.

The typical summer house rises six to eight feet above the ground on sturdy wooden pillars that are topped by a wooden floor. Above this floor by only about five feet is a thatched roof. The deck itself measures approximately 8' x 8'. To enter the deck house, one climbs a ladder and crawls onto the deck. The deck house is surprisingly sturdy, but it does sway in the wind or when a newcomer climbs in.

The Yami enjoy sleeping in their deck houses on hot summer nights. The night winds are cool and keep the insects away. The ocean, seldom more than a couple hundred feet away, raises the soothing sound of gentle surf. Birds can be heard in the mountain woodlands, and in some villages the sound of a waterfall carries across the grassland at night. Men often nap in the summer house on hot afternoons, sometimes taking along the smallest child in the family. While I was on Lan-yu, I was given the use of a summer house. Looking out from my perch I could see the blue Pacific and nearby perplexing rock formations. The gentle breeze added to my sense of peace during the time I spent there.

While this three-house arrangement is typical, it is not universal. Poorer families do not have all three houses; but the arrangement is an ideal to which the Yami aspire, and many reach it. These three houses fit the Lan-yu environment, and the arrangement has evolved from reasonable needs and desires to live and work on the island. But the houses also convey status, just as a fine house in any Western country might denote its owner's social and economic standing.

Observing how the Yami live should give one pause to consider one's own lifestyle. I am reminded of Ruth Benedict's comment in her book, *Patterns of Culture* (1934): "It is one of the philosophical justifications for the study of primitive peoples that the facts of simpler cultures may make clear social facts that are otherwise baffling and not open to demonstration."

29

Chapter Five

YAMI SPIRITUALITY

Previously in this study, I mentioned that the Yami believe in spirits, or ghosts; for example, they sanctify, or "cleanse," the beach of demons before firing pottery. The religion of the Yami is ghost worship. This religion dominates every waking moment of Yami life, much as demon and angel beliefs ruled the minds of medieval folk during Europe's Dark Ages. Foreign religions have never made headway on the island.

The Yami see their world as the center of the universe and themselves as the chosen people. Although missionaries have attempted to convert them, most Yami, though polite to church people, have not accepted Christian or Buddhist notions. Only one small Buddhist shrine can be found on the island, and its presence is merely symbolic: to remind visitors and the locals that Lan-yu is now part of China. Unless it is pointed out, a visitor probably never would notice it.

The foundation of the Yami's beliefs is not dissimilar to many creation stories. Their creation story is about how God chose their island of Lan-yu as his most special place. It is said that God was searching the earth and seas, and he looked down from on high and saw Lan-yu, an island of beauty and peace. Thus he decided to populate it. God let fall a large boulder from the heavens, and it landed atop a high mountain on Lan-yu. Because of its size and roundness, it rolled down the slope to settle in the valley below. He then sent down a large shoot of bamboo that, because of its lightness in the wind, landed not on the mountain peak but rather on the flat land at the edge of the island. Both the boulder and the bamboo shoot split open. From the boulder emerged a boy; from the bamboo, a girl. And they were the first Yami people.

The story goes on that the sun was so powerful on Lan-yu that God gave the Yami morning mist, which created dew and provided them with drink. As the boy grew up, he wanted children. He rubbed his right knee, and he gave birth to a son; by rubbing his left knee, he was given a daughter. Girls, it is said, came out of the left side because it is weaker, while boys came out of the right side. God also sent them all of the animals and plants they would need to live happily, and the man gave the flora and fauna names and showed the children their uses. The children of the man then began to marry one another and to produce children through sexual relations, but their offspring were all blind or ill because they were all brothers and sisters. Only when the man from the boulder and woman from the bamboo required their children to marry outside their family circle did healthy offspring emerge.

This story also says that when it was time to give birth, the man would sharpen his ax and open the woman; the woman always died. However, over time, by observing how the she-goat gave birth, the woman learned that if she pushed hard when her time came, then the baby would come out healthy. She therefore forbade the man from using his ax to open her stomach and take out the infant.

The creation story of the Yami, which is passed down from generation to generation, deals with a number of eternal questions and, in its simplicity, answers the issue on their origin and also presents a strong argument for the taboo of incest. Even today, though their population is small, men and women who are related are forbidden to marry. Most find their mates in neighboring villages and the other clans.

In spite of this creation story, which is not dissimilar to the stories of other peoples not only in the Pacific but elsewhere, the day-to-day spiritual obsession among the Yami is with ghosts, which are universally feared. This fear of ghosts dominates much of Yami life, a point that I will reiterate in future chapters. Ghost worship practices and superstitions are not readily apparent to the casual observer. But anyone who lives for a time among the Yami comes to see how their belief in ghosts literally haunts them in their day-to-day pursuits.

On my first day on Lan-yu, I came across an old man from one of the villages. He was dressed in battle attire. A metal helmet with eye holes covered most of his head and extended down to his shoulders; and he carried a stout, long, curved sword of iron with a wooden handle. (Yami men often carry ornamental daggers, too. They are the only aboriginal tribe of Taiwan that wear battle armor.)

It was sunset as I watched this man walk along a path. Every few paces he would fiercely swing his broad sword, striking at the air around him. Knowing no better, I assumed that the man was either mentally disturbed or had been drinking. Fortunately, I was able to check my assumption — and found that I was wrong. My host that evening was the principal of the Chinese junior high school on the island, who asked the man about his behavior.

The problem, the man said, was that he was plagued by ghosts. They bothered him all day long and became particularly bothersome during the evening hours. By swinging his sword, the old man could keep at bay the ghosts that seemed determined to make his life miserable.

Ghosts, according to Yami beliefs, are demonic spirits from beyond death's door who have returned to earth to terrorize the people of Lan-yu. For example, among the most evil such ghosts are the spirits of those who have died from starvation, particularly if they were actively denied food or care; they will return to seek vengeance on the living. The Yami believe that ghosts are most likely to appear on nights when the moon is full. Therefore, few Yami will venture from the safety of their homes on such nights. Men who must travel between villages wear metal helmets and carry swords. Should a man feel the presence of a ghost, he will draw his blade and swing it about to protect himself, just as did the old man whom I encountered. Children can be seen sleeping with daggers, because the Yami believe that iron can ward off ghosts.

Ghosts also appear in dreams. In this way they communicate their intentions. A person who has a particularly gruesome dream may stay in the main house for weeks without venturing forth. Dreams, the Yami believe, both anticipate the future and interpret the past. The Yami routinely tell one another about their dreams and perform rituals to mitigate their fears.

Some rituals are exceedingly strange. For example, if a woman gives birth to twins, the second child is immediately killed because the Yami fear that it will be possessed. Handicapped children are similarly eliminated for fear that they are, in reality, ghostly beings.

When I first visited Lan-yu, my initial impression was of a people living in paradise. While the lives of the Yami did not seem carefree, the people at least seemed happy with their lot and productive within the confines of their island culture. The men setting out in their ocean-going canoes were determined and brave. Only gradually did I come to see the fear and superstition that often are crippling. Breaking a taboo, using the wrong totem, failing to follow a custom — all might lead to death or insanity, according to the Yami belief system.

I mentioned previously that Little Orchid Island (or Little Lan-yu), the atoll to the north, is said to be possessed by ghosts. It is taboo. Although some men go there, it is largely avoided — and feared. Other taboos and superstitions seem limitless: Men may eat only certain types of fish; women only others. Special small houses are built for pregnant women, so that they can be isolated. A woman who has given birth may not go to the seashore for a year. Houses may contain nothing that is pointed; this would bring bad luck. Certain words may not be uttered because they will bring bad luck. The number 4 is particularly unlucky. And the list goes on and on.

As might be supposed, death is an event riddled with fear and foreboding. The Yami have no belief in a life after death. And the Yami never speak of death. They go to great lengths to protect themselves from dying or being near a dying person; when a death occurs, the experience is wiped from memory as quickly as possible. In fact, burial may occur in anticipation of death, so great is the Yami fear of having a dead body near them. If an old person becomes sick and the family believes that he or she will soon die, they dig a hole near the ocean; the individual may be buried even before he or she breathes a final breath. A relative who dies and is not quickly buried may haunt the living for years.

The person who dies suddenly or is killed in an accident is buried immediately. Fishermen lost at sea are believed to float back to Lan-yu to walk the island as ghosts. The Yami hold no burial ceremonies, nor do they mark the graves of their dead. There are no discussions about the dead person's life or accomplishments. The dead are effectively taboo. And should a dead body be washed out to sea after being buried on the shore, the event is regarded as a terrible omen. If a body washes back on the shore, it is immediately reburied.

The Yami fear of ghosts is a contradiction, a dark shadow across the seeming paradise of Lan-yu. Yami men and women routinely walk miles out of their way to avoid being near a burial site. The power of their beliefs shapes the Yami way of life in ways that are deeper than can be seen by the casual observer. Because these beliefs have persisted, even grown, over centuries, they also have played — and continue to play — a key role in shaping Yami survival in today's world and the changing character of their culture.

Chapter Six

GROWING UP YAMI

The Yami have remained a homogeneous people, because Lan-yu until recently has been largely isolated from outside contact. No political powers in the area have ever regarded Lan-yu as a possession of any importance. Therefore few outsiders have ever bothered to visit Lan-yu. Intermarriage with non-Yami still is virtually unknown *on* the island (although a few Yami seek partners off the island). As a result of this close breeding (not inbreeding), the Yami have maintained a distinctive physical appearance.

Both genetic disposition and a life in the sun render the Yami skin a dark brown. Only infants are paler, until they toddle out to play on the beaches. As adults, both Yami men and women tend to be strongly built with powerful shoulders and backs, which make their short legs seem even smaller by comparison. Indeed, in stature the Yami are the shortest among the Taiwan aboriginal groups. Men average about 5'5", women a few inches shorter.

A Yami child is born in a specially constructed, isolated hut, which the Yami refer to as a "birth room." This structure is constructed by the child's father and his male relatives as soon as the mother-to-be's pregnancy is discovered. Once the pregnant woman moves into the hut, usually about two months before the birth is expected, men are no longer allowed to enter. A midwife helps the mother to deliver, and the umbilical cord is cut with a sharpened piece of bamboo. The newborn is immediately immersed in cold water, dried off, and then wrapped in soft material. Later, the baby's body will be oiled, and the baby will be nursed.

As I noted in Chapter Five, deformed babies and the second of twins are killed at birth, though I was told that such events occurred only rarely. However, unlike in several other Asian societies, notably mainland China, boys and girls are desired equally.

After a birth the mother is allowed to rest for three days; on the fourth day she resumes her regular activities and moves back to the main house. Mothers may continue to nurse their infants for two to four years or until the mother becomes pregnant again. But in any event the infant is nursed for at least a year. If a mother is working in the fields, then her baby is brought to her to nurse during the workday. And at night, baby and mother share the same bed.

The infants of most working mothers are looked after by aunts, grandmothers, or friends. Babies are rarely allowed to cry. At the first peep, someone will pick up the baby and rock it and sing to it. Later, when the babies become toddlers, they will be looked after mostly by older children. It is not uncommon to see a little girl of five or so carrying an even younger brother or sister, feeding the toddler, and sleeping on the same mat.

Babies are kept scrupulously clean. Each main house features a large wooden or iron tub in the front yard, and children seem to be constantly dunked into this water to ensure their cleanliness. Whenever the weather is warm, which is nearly always, babies are left unclothed. Diapers are not used. Regular washing prevents illness, rashes, odors, and the like.

Unfortunately, in spite of this commitment to cleanliness, the Yami experience a high rate of infant mortality (apart from infanticides). About 40% of Yami infants die within the first year of life. In fact, life expectancy among the Yami on the whole is relatively short. While the Chinese population of nearby Taiwan has the same life expectancy as Europeans and Americans, the Yami are not so fortunate. Childhood diseases, stomach ailments (ulcers and cancer), dehydration, diarrhea, and accidents claim a large

Two of the littlest Yami enjoy bathtime. Children, who wear no clothing until puberty, are kept very clean. Baths are frequent.

percentage of the infants and young children. Once a Yami reaches age five, his or her chances of living to age 55 improve. Life expectancy for men is slightly higher than for women because of the significant number of women who die during childbirth.

Children of both sexes live without clothing until puberty (age nine for most girls; age ten for boys). Young children are allowed great freedom to play on the beaches, in the fields, and on the hillsides. Once puberty arrives, boys copy their fathers' dress and don a kind of loincloth. Girls adopt the dress of their mothers, a loose skirt and blouse. (Red is a favorite color for girls and women.) Modesty in dress for adults is a community standard.

Interestingly, during the 1970s the Taiwanese government opened a public elementary school for the Yami children. The school requires students to wear standard school uniforms; but the moment the youngsters are home, they hop out of their European-style pants or skirts.

The Yami exemplify the notion that it takes a village to raise a child. Sharing is an important tenet of Yami life, and privacy is almost unknown. Any item in any house may be borrowed and used by anyone in the village. The Yami have no word for stealing. And this attitude extends to child care. Children are allowed to run free, to enter any home, and to help themselves to food and other items. They are watched over by everyone in the community. If a child gets tired, he or she simply goes to the nearest house, opens the door, and lies down on an empty bed. Any family that comes home to find a child in their house will care for the child. The child may even stay for several days with this "aunt" or "uncle." And, because crimes against children are unheard of, no parents worry much when their son or daughter is away from home.

Discipline, like stealing, is an unknown concept. Yami children are never scolded or punished. What might seem to be annoying or obnoxious behavior to a Western parent is considered simply to be normal behavior for children. As a result, Yami children invariably smile and seem happy. They eat when they are hungry, sleep when they are tired, chase butterflies, search for seashells,

40

catch birds, and make noise from dawn until dusk. Also, children are rarely alone. From early years onward, children play in groups of five to ten, running wildly on the beach and through the village.

Early group bonding and almost unlimited freedom build a sense of group spirit, or community, which is characteristic of Yami society. Yami men and women band together to confront challenges with vigor and determination bolstered by a high sense of cooperation and camaraderie that begins in childhood.

The Yami sense of sharing was brought home to me when I offered a cigarette to an old woman. The woman smoked only half of the cigarette and then extinguished it. I was curious. She told me that she planned to save the other half for her husband, who was at their summer house minding their grandchildren.

As children grow to adulthood, childhood nudity gives way to standard clothing, as I mentioned previously. But even as adults the Yami wear few clothes. And, unlike many other aboriginal groups, they do not use tattoos for personal ornamentation. However, they do adorn themselves with such things as elaborate hats, ear pendants, necklaces or chest ornaments, and wrist and leg bracelets. Jewelry items most often are made of shells or silver, but seeds, wild boars' teeth, and fish bones also are popular. Perhaps the most-favored decorative item is the nautilus shell, which is admired by both men and women.

Beginning in adolescence a number of customs and taboos become evident. For example, when a girl begins menstruating, she is isolated from activities involving boys and men. During a menstrual period, a girl must stay in her house and avoid all contact with males.

As body hair begins to appear, both boys and girls are initiated into Yami hair-removal practices. The Yami do not like body hair, which they remove by plucking. The Yami are similar to most Asians in that they seldom have much body hair to begin with, but underarm and pubic hair is carefully removed. Yami men also remove facial hair and have the hair on their head cut monthly. The preferred style is to leave the hair on the top of the head full and to shave the head from about mid-ear downward. Unlike most of their Asian neighbors, the Yami usually have rather bushy or kinky hair, rather than straight hair. And their hair often is reddish-brown or even somewhat golden, rather than black, the result, I was told, of vitamin deficiencies common to a number of Pacific islanders.

Yami society is clan-centric, and so great stress is laid on maintaining good relations with relatives and between clans. With only six clan villages on Lan-yu, it is easy to see that such an attitude also is a practical necessity. Marriage matches must be made between different clans, because marriage between related individuals is one of the strictest taboos.

Unlike parents in most Asian and Western societies, Yami parents have no particular aspirations for their children. Expectations for children to grow up and attend college, travel, or become wealthy or famous are not on the Yami parenting agenda. But marriage most assuredly is. In fact, only marriage formally marks the end of childhood. Most men marry at 22 or 23; women at 16 or 17. Marriage is considered to be both important and wonderful. Monogamy is the rule.

Most marriages are arranged by the parents, some betrothing their children as early as in infancy. Although in recent years romantic love has become a greater factor in one's choice of a marriage partner, a large percentage of marriages still are contracted; and the likelihood of clandestine relationships outside the marriage contract is reduced by the small size of the Yami population and their close-knit community. Indeed, the Yami may be characterized as puritanical in most sexual-relationship matters, in contrast to what may be witnessed in aboriginal groups on Taiwan itself. The engagement of a man to a woman is a formal contract, and both families must agree. Either family can veto the decision.

When a man formally asks a woman to marry him, he presents her with five to seven pieces of round, highly polished, valuable coral. Usually the man has found the coral himself and then had the coral cut and polished professionally. Coral is regarded as a jewel, and visitors to Asia will notice that it plays a significant role in the economy of numerous cultures. The Yami man's gift is a token of his pledge to marry, and the coral will be returned to him if the engagement falls through or the couple later divorces. On accepting the gift of coral, the woman will display it proudly to her family and friends.

An interesting feature of Yami life inserts itself into the marriage equation: the power of women. This power arises, in part, from the fact that there are fewer women than men on Lan-yu. But other factors contribute. For example, property rights and custody of children favor women. If a man behaves badly or simply proves to be a poor spouse, then the woman can tell him to leave the house and can unilaterally divorce him (though divorce is rare). Men, therefore, must be attractive, hardworking, and kind if they want to succeed in wooing a Yami bride.

When I visited the island in 1994, an old Yami woman told me, "The women of Lan-yu must be strong because men have so many weaknesses." Men of unblemished reputation from a good family have the best chance of success in courtship. And, in the Yami mind, only women of the island are worth marrying. The man who fails to win a wife on Lan-yu is faced with the prospect of searching for a mate among the other tribes in Taiwan. Thus a Yami man works hard to prove his worthiness as a husband. Women, on the other hand, attract men by their physical appearance as much as by any other characteristic. Beauty in a woman consists of fair skin; large eyes; dark, curly, long hair; prominent breasts; good posture, and cleanliness.

The Yami have a distinctive version of romantic love that appears to be a meld of their traditions and influences from the Japanese and Chinese. Television, a relatively recent addition to island life, will likely alter the Yami sense of romantic love as time goes by.

Women take the lead in courtship. Both men and women give gifts during courtship; necklaces, woodcarvings, and food are often exchanged. Horseplay between men and women (and boys and girls) prior to marriage is seen as natural and helpful in allowing members of the opposite sex to adjust to communication and physical interaction. For a woman to touch a man's genitals is not considered shameful.

I would note that homosexuality is not evident among the Yami, though it may exist. However, same-sex contact between women is often seen. Women frequently touch or caress one another, and they dance together on ritual occasions, which are frequent on the island.

Marriage day on Lan-yu is tradition-bound. At sunrise on the day of the marriage, the mother of the groom goes to the bride's house and escorts the bride to her son's house, usually a very simple structure. (Later on, as they are able, the couple will build the three houses that I described in Chapter Four.) A large feast is held, featuring dishes of pork, chicken, and goat. At this feast the groom and bride promise to live as husband and wife before the assembled wellwishers. The couple's parents and other relatives acknowledge the bond, and the couple begins a life together. Children are expected within the first two years of marriage.

Incidentally, this festive occasion is not marked by alcohol consumption. The Yami do not use alcohol. I have been told by Chinese ethnologists that a majority of the marital problems seen among aboriginal groups in Taiwan can be directly traced to substance abuse, mainly the abuse of alcohol. Surely the absence of alcohol must be one reason for the low divorce rate among the Yami. They are one of the few Asian groups that does not produce wine or beer.

After the marriage ceremony a young man will continue to work closely with his father. Similarly, a woman also will maintain a close tie to her family, which is in contrast to the practice seen in most Chinese and Japanese cultures. Fathers and sons enjoy working together and relish, in particular, the fishing expeditions that are so important to their culture. (The "boat culture" aspect of Yami life I have reserved for a fuller treatment in Chapter Eight.) A new wife will share her time with her husband, her new in-laws, and her parents and other relatives as needed.

I have said that the Yami may be considered almost puritanical in sexual matters. Although children run about naked most of the time, the Yami are reticent about nudity and sexual matters. Modesty both before and after marriage is the rule. Newlyweds are particularly shy. Girls seldom hear anything about sexuality until marriage, when an aunt or sister may take them aside for a serious conversation. I cannot recall ever seeing a husband and wife holding hands during my visits to Lan-yu. Public displays of affection are against custom, and adult nudity is rare even in the home. In fact, many men never see their wives totally unclothed throughout their marriage.

Sexual congress is said to be far less frequent than is the case in most cultures. To some extent this may be blamed on a combination of sexual reticence and lack of privacy. Because living spaces often are shared, married couples usually wait until they think everyone else in the room is asleep before engaging in intercourse. Then either husband or wife may indicate sexual desire by caressing the other. Kissing and oral-genital contact are not part of the romantic paradigm of the Yami. Touching takes their place. Intercourse is performed in traditional positions, usually under blankets or shawls.

Women further exert their power by denying their husbands sexual activity as punishment, usually related to some lack of success in fishing, boat building, or home construction. As I mentioned earlier, the onus is on the man to measure up to the woman's expectations. If a woman should divorce a man, she will readily find another husband. The man may not be so lucky.

Although Yami society is egalitarian, clearly some families are more successful than others. In the more successful families, the oldest son can anticipate inheriting both property and status at the death of his father. His mother will become his charge in her old age and will be cared for in the family home. The smallness of the island ensures that people will see their kinfolk on a daily basis; loneliness is not a problem for the Yami.

Before I close this chapter on growing up Yami, I should say a little more about health and nutrition. The vitamin deficiency that colors their hair is only one problem, along with infanticide and a variety of life-threatening illnesses, that contributes to the short life expectancy of the Yami. Green vegetables and fruits are in short supply. Vitamin C deficiencies are particularly prevalent, as are deficiencies of numerous minerals that simply do not exist in the island foods.

The main ailment in infancy is enteritis that, unchecked, leads to death. I noted previously that if a child reaches age five, then he or she has a vastly increased chance of surviving to adulthood. However, stomach and intestinal illnesses also occur with high frequency in adulthood. Stomach and colon cancers, liver dysfunction, and infections that result from injuries are all too common. On the other hand, sexually transmitted diseases are almost unknown on Lan-yu. They occur only if a Yami man or woman has lived off the island and then returned.

Skin problems also are common among the Yami. Skin cancer, a result of constant exposure to the sun, is prevalent. Some other island peoples (for example, the Pung-hu, who live on the west side of Taiwan) take pains to cover themselves while fishing or working in the fields, but this is not the case with the Yami. Constant exposure to wind and sun renders young skin old within a few years. As I traveled about the island, I also noticed many individuals with open sores which appeared to be the result of minor injuries but, because of constant exposure and lack of medicine, could not heal. Leg wounds appear rather common, as do foot injuries and abrasions. The latter result from going about barefooted.

It is easy to see that the Yami life is a mixture of happiness and hardship. Modern medicines and health care hold the potential for improving their quality of life, but increased contact with the world beyond Lan-yu also is fraught with peril. Off-islanders can as easily bring disease as education, or prosperity, or material goods. And television, just now becoming a factor, has the potential for transforming the Yami culture. Will it bring greater happiness or the opposite?

Chapter
Seven

A DAY'S WORK

Work on Lan-yu, as elsewhere, is a primary basis for society and culture. Virtually all Yami work at something, the main tasks being boat building, fishing, farming, construction, and food preparation. All healthy adults are expected to work; and for men, as I pointed out in Chapter Six, worth and status — particularly as a marriageable bachelor — are created by work.

Children learn about work by watching their parents, unlike in more "advanced" societies where children and adults spend much of their time apart. But boys and girls are not required to work, even though they often are eager to try their hand at the tasks their elders perform. Indeed, a childlike eagerness characterizes the general approach of the Yami to work. Even community leaders, high-status individuals, pitch in on projects involving manual labor. When hard work is necessary, it is done with enthusiasm. Individuals who are lazy are viewed as sick and are shunned by others.

Day breaks early on Lan-yu, especially on the eastern side of the island. But even before dawn the Yami are up and about. The first of their two daily meals is breakfast. Hot yams or taro root are popular breakfast foods, occasionally accompanied by smoked flying fish. Children enjoy hot, sweetened goat's milk. I never saw any Yami drink coffee or tea. Nor have Chinese dietary habits found their way to Lan-yu. They do not eat rice or other cereal grains. (Interestingly enough, my Yami hosts prepared Chinese meals for me during my stay. Even though I was a Westerner, they figured I was closer to being Chinese than Yami.)

Following the washing up after breakfast, the adults in each village set to work. Tasks for men and women are clearly defined. The women walk down dirt paths to small fields where the island's crops are grown. These fields fill the land that stretches between the beaches and the mountains and belong to clans, rather than to individuals. The crops consist mainly of sweet potatoes, taro root, water potatoes, and some wheat-related grains. Fruit trees are rare on Lan-yu. Occasionally one can find very small, bitter oranges; and wild berries can be picked here and there.

Women are the island's farmers, and their chores include planting, weeding, irrigating, and harvesting. They also tend livestock: pigs, goats, chickens, and a few other animals. Because the Yami have no formal monetary system, none of the crops are sold. Rather, trading and borrowing are means for exchanging goods. Generosity abounds. When an individual or boat group has good luck fishing, the catch is shared among all the family members and beyond. The same is true for a good harvest. Hoarding is unheard of, for no Yami wants to be responsible for the starvation of another, whose ghost — the worst of all ghosts — may return to seek revenge.

Although they usually wear large reed hats, Yami women do not clothe themselves as thoroughly as Chinese farm women, who normally are covered from head to toe. Because of the long exposure to the hot equatorial sun, a Yami woman in her mid-twenties will have the leathery skin of a much older person. Women actually are exposed to the harsh sunlight somewhat more than men, whose jobs often can be done in shade — with the exception of fishing. Men can frequently be found in the main house or the "social house," working on projects, watching over the many children running about the village, or smoking tobacco. The child-minding activities are shared with older members of the community.

After a morning of working in the field, building boats, or constructing houses, Yami men and women return home. They may bathe in the ocean or a convenient stream and then relax as the midday heat sears the island. Men usually nap in the summer house (or "deck house"), bringing their youngest child up the ladder with them to catch the cooling breeze under the thatched roof. Women busy themselves in the main house, where they begin to make preparations for the second of the two daily meals. This second meal will be eaten in late afternoon.

I am not certain why the Yami follow a two-meal-a-day dietary plan. It seems to have been set in place during the 1900s, but whether from lack of time or lack of food is difficult to determine. At any rate, dinner, like breakfast, is eaten by the entire family, normally sitting on rocks or squatting in the courtyard of the main house. Children continue to play and are fed "on the run" as the adults eat. A hungry child is allowed to "borrow" food from anyone. Fish, yams, and other dishes are eaten mostly with the fingers; the Yami do not use chopsticks.

During meals, older men are given preference in the selection of foods and are served first. The Yami enjoy talking and joking, telling tales and adventures, as they eat. The Yami genuinely enjoy one another's company. Mealtime is a good time for sharing stories about times at sea, failures in farming, love and marriage, and plans for the future and gossiping about their own and the other Yami villages. Each Yami views his or her own village as best, and the Yami generally divide the world into only two groups: Yami and non-Yami. Non-Yami are seen as spoilers of culture and tradition and also as "modernizers," a Yami euphemism for those who would commit cultural genocide.

After dinner both men and women join in clean-up chores.

The Yami world on Lan-yu is literally timeless. Clocks do not exist, nor do written records. Their calendar was devised centuries ago and is primitive by Western standards. Sunrise signals the beginning of the day; sunset, a time for quiet and sleep. Months are 30 days long. A year consists of 12 months. And every third year the Yami insert a 60-day month to adjust the calendar to match the perceived seasons.

For the Yami there are only three seasons, which coincide with the prevailing weather patterns and also are based on a cycle of farming and fishing. "Summer" (in Western terms) stretches from about July through October. Farming is most extensive during this season. Women, the farmers, are most active during this period; men spend much of their time in the summer house.

"Winter" sets in during November, when the weather changes noticeably. Temperatures fall into the 50s. The winds increase in strength, and rain falls almost every day. The Yami spend most of their time in the main house during this season. They work on repairing fishing equipment and tend to household chores. The wind is so strong during the winter that it can tear apart a house that is not strongly built, and even strong houses demand repairs. Few people venture out except by necessity, and the winding paths from village to village are deserted except for children going to school.

"Spring" — from March through June — is the most exciting season for the Yami. The harsh winter days give way to sunny breezes, and people emerge from the main houses to enjoy the new season. If summer is the heavy work time for women, for men that time is spring. Much male labor is directed toward fishing — spring is called "Flying Fish Season" — and that goes on until the final harvest in July.

I should point out, however, that seasonal work overlaps. Some farming goes on year-round, as does some fishing to a lesser extent. And there are always houses to be built, boats to be constructed, and indoor work to be done.

Another fact of Yami life is governance, which functions at three levels: family, village (clan), and island. I have stated previously that women have significant power and influence in matters associated with the family. This contrasts with the circumstances in which most Asian women find themselves. Women broaden their influence through a sense of camaraderie that comes of long hours working in the fields together and the natural bonding with one another as they share in rituals, dance activities, the upbringing of children, and so on. Such bonding makes them a political force with which to be reckoned.

Each village has a male leader (or elder) who coordinates activities, particularly boat building and fishing. These elders become the island's spokesmen on matters that involve the Taiwanese authorities, who maintain a small government outpost on Lan-yu. Common discussion themes include concerns about pollution, education, military service for Yami men, and unwanted tourism. On rare occasions the Yami leaders have gathered in full battle regalia and marched on various government ministries in Taipei to present grievances. But the Yami goal in most discussions with the Taiwan government is to retain their independence and to maintain their way of life. In particular, the Yami view modernization as detrimental to their traditional values and destructive to their island environment.

The casual visitor to Lan-yu will find it difficult to understand the dynamic at work in Yami culture. The Yami have no written history, and no reliable Western studies have been done on this aboriginal group. (Wu Che-gung's 1986 book about the Yami, in Chinese, can be helpful, though it is not readily accessible to the English-speaking public.) To outsiders on first meeting, the Yami seem rather vain and arrogant. They walk very erect, give full attention to whatever task is at hand, and seem unimpressed, even uninterested, in visitors walking about their villages. And, in fact, they are a noble people who have mastered their island life and are largely self-sufficient. But when one delves deeper, one finds them to be a close-knit community that maintains high standards of conduct and that values human relationships and interactions.

Tourism, to some extent, has engendered a new behavior: begging. The visitor to Lan-yu is quickly surrounded by children with outstretched hands. Candy and gum are greatly appreciated. Adult Yami like to receive cigarettes, which make an appropriate greeting or thank-you gift.

Yami begging has some roots in the period of Japanese control, when the Yami no doubt were given gifts to reward them for musical and dance performances. The Yami thus associate gifts with foreign visitors, and the Yami associate the ability to visit Lan-yu with wealth. Visitors can afford to give the Yami things they cannot otherwise obtain. Another factor further contributes to Yami begging, which is the Yami practice of sharing and borrowing. The "what's mine is yours" attitude is extended through begging to outsiders. And because trading is a way of life for the Yami, there has developed a sense that trading candy or cigarettes for the privilege of traveling from village to village and talking with families also is acceptable practice in dealing with outsiders.

Finally, money — traditionally foreign to Yami society — is now beginning to be seen.

Chapter
Eight

BOAT CULTURE

I have reserved this chapter for a discussion of boat culture, because it is the most distinctive feature of Yami culture. Every aspect of boat building and fishing is laden with ritual and superstition. So great is the mystique surrounding this activity that it may be said that the Yami are defined by the boat and all it symbolizes. Certainly the boat culture sets the Yami apart from other Taiwan aboriginal groups.

When one visits Lan-yu, one cannot help but be drawn to the stunningly beautiful ocean-going canoes that are beached near each of the Yami villages. In the Western world a person's house or car may convey status. In the Yami world status is convey by the family's boat. Once a Yami man builds a boat, he rises in status. The successful Yami man points to his boat, his wife and children, and his three houses as the emblems of his success and prosperity. But boat culture does not end there. The boat also symbolizes a way of life, for fishing is all-important to Yami men, whose families otherwise would be reduced to subsisting on the crops brought in from the fields by their womenfolk. The boat's importance makes it the closest token that the Yami have as a symbol of worship. Festivals for launching assume the trappings of religious ceremonies.

In addition to my own observations on Lan-yu, I have drawn on two important pieces of scholarship to write this chapter. First are the writings of Tadao Kano. His article, "Lan-yu: Boat Building Ceremony," appeared in a 1938 issue of *Human Culture* magazine. A later article, "South Asian Boat Building," appeared in 1946 in the *Southeast Asia Journal*. Unfortunately, both articles are available only in Japanese. The second is a somewhat shorter but useful treatment written by the Chinese scholar Jeng Huey-Ing, "The Yami Boat Culture," which appeared in a 1984 issue of the Chinese-language *Bulletin of Ethnology*. This article, in part, summarizes (and condenses) the work of Tadao Kano. Its major contribution is the commentary on the modern pressures that the Yami were facing as of the early 1980s. Sadly, no major works on Yami boat culture have been published in English.

It seems reasonable to begin with the construction of an ocean-going canoe. For as long as they have existed as a people, the Yami have built their boats from the native woods that grow on the island. When a man and his family decide to build a boat, the first task is to find just the right woods. The best trees are found in the highlands and, once located, are marked with a family insignia. A shaman is consulted about the best day to cut the timber, and prayers are offered to make the canoe strong and safe before the first cut of the ax is ever made.

All of the woods are indigenous to the Pacific, if not exclusively to Lan-yu. The first wood selected will be for the bow and stern. Hard, heavy lumber is needed for these sections. The *Neonauclea reticulata* is preferred. When such a tree is felled, the curved sections that will be fitted together to form the bow and stern are skillfully cut out. The Yami do not bend the wood. Rather, the desired shape is obtained by carving, using small axes, knives, and draw planes.

The Yami build two types of canoes. A large, or "grand," canoe is constructed using 27 planks and will carry 6, 8, 10, or 12 men. A small canoe is constructed using fewer than 21 planks and will carry one, two, or three men. Readers may recall that the number 4 is unlucky to the Yami; no canoe is ever built to carry four men.

Taboos about women also are enforced. Women — particularly pregnant women — are not permitted to come to the construction site.

When a man and his male relatives build a canoe, that team must be together at the building site only on the first day of construction. Thereafter, individuals will choose to work as needed. A hard day of work may be followed by several days of rest. In this way it takes three years to complete a grand canoe. August is the month when boat building is begun, because the fishing season is over and the days are hot. A man may work on his boat for a while and then climb up to the deck of his summer house for a smoke. Contemplating the next stage of building over cigarettes on a sunny afternoon is a common practice.

While the wood for the bow and stern is most important, the lumber for the remainder of the boat is not inconsequential. The external hull planks at and below sea level are cut from *Garcinia linii*, which is not quite as hard as the bow and stern wood but still is heavy and strong. This type of timber is found throughout the Indo-Malaysian region and may be compared to the laubu tree in the Fiji Islands and the gatasan tree in the Philippines. Remaining parts of the boat will be made from *Hibiscus mutabilis* (known as a cotton-rose or Confederate-rose in the United States), a softer, lighter wood that cuts easily. By choosing these woods, the Yami create a bottom-heavy craft that does not need a centerboard or keel.

A remarkable feature of Yami boat building is that the planks are cut without using markings or blueprints. In fact, the 27 planks are cut independently. And yet, when the boat is assembled, everything will fit together with only a small amount of final shaving.

Assembly begins with another ritual. The master boat builder kills a chicken and splashes its blood on the joints and edges that will fit together to ensure their integrity. Then the boat is assembled using no metal at all. Mortise-and-tenon joints are used for the bow and stern. The main planks are fitted together with lapjoints, and hardwood pegs are forced into pre-drilled holes to

Yami women perform ritual dances in celebration of the launching of the new grand canoe, an event that takes place only once every five years or so.

The male Yami in this photo are participating in a ritual designed to repel demons and ghosts. They grimace, blow out their cheeks, and shake their fists to ensure that the new boat will remain free of evil spirits.

Children imitate their fathers and mothers during the festivities of the boat launching.

Totems of dried chicken feathers decorate the stern and bow of the new grand canoe.

Men carry a new boat toward the shoreline in preparation for launching it.

Before the new grand canoe is set gently in the water, the Yami men ritually toss it into the air and catch it three times.

secure the planks. Each piece of wood is fitted tightly against its neighbor so that, when the water swells the wood, each joint and space will be tight. Cotton tree fibers are used to fill any large remaining spaces. The result is an ocean-worthy craft that cannot be paralleled in the Pacific.

I should mention that metal, motor-driven boats were introduced to the island in the 1970s. Some Yami use these powered boats, but the boats are held in no special regard and have no status value. Indeed, the lack of enthusiasm for these "modern" boats is evident in their shabby appearance. Most of the metal boats I saw were battered and in a state of disrepair.

For a magnificent wooden canoe, the next step in the building process is painting. Although cutting and assembling a boat is complex, perhaps the most sophisticated aspect of boat building is painting. First, totems for luck and safety are carved on the hull. Then red, white, and black paints are used to create overall designs. In the old days the paints were made using berries, soot, powdered seashells, and other natural colorants mixed with tree sap; but now the Yami use waterproof paints that are commercially available. After the paint has dried and the wood has had a chance to season, the boat will be filled with water to swell the joints and pegs.

To complete a boat, seats are added, along with oar braces and securing lines made from hemp, and paddles are carved. Each decorated paddle is made from two pieces of wood: a shaft about five feet long and a flat blade secured to the shaft with wooden pegs. A wooden extension also is constructed and fitted to hold a rudder to the right of the center of the canoe. This rudder will be used by a helmsman, who will steer the canoe as it is rowed.

As the boat is being finished, word is sent to the other villages. Completion, particularly of a grand canoe, is heralded with great fanfare and feasting. A festival takes place that will last two days and reach its zenith with the launching of the new boat. No event in Yami cultural life draws more interest and involvement than the launching of a new canoe. Yami from every village will participate.

The festival is planned to coincide with a full moon. The boat builder and his relatives provide all of the food for this event. For days, even weeks, prior to the festival women and children will be seen in the fields harvesting food, particularly taro root, which they gather by the hundreds into large sacks to take to the festival site. Taro root, which is similar to the sweet potato, is served in great quantities along with pork, goat, and chicken. The revelers sing and perform ritual dances in between periods of feasting.

Finally, the great day arrives: the beginning of the launching festival. Literally thousands of taro roots are mounded on the canoe until only the highest parts — bow and stern — remain visible. The roots that it took women weeks to gather are made into this mountain by the men, who will take the most important roles in the launching ritual. To show their respect on the launching of a new boat, all the men from the various villages will don their armor. Dressed in leather vest, loincloth, and metal helmet and carrying a lance, they will gather to sing ritual songs (many dating back centuries) and shout praises of the canoe builders. Women will perform ritual dances. Toward the end of the first day, some of the guests will return home; others will remain to smoke, eat, and tell stories.

The festival really gets under way on the second day. Taro roots are taken from the great mound and cooked. Pigs brought from the various villages are slaughtered, and both blood and flesh are cooked to be eaten during the festival period. Care is taken to ensure that everyone gets an equal share of the food and is included in the singing and dancing. Children run wild, and everyone has a good time.

About the middle of the second day, the men put on their ceremonial armor again. They surround the boat, which now has been cleared of taro root. And then the entire adult male assembly lifts the boat off its stand and raises it high above their heads. This act in itself is dangerous and awe-inspiring. A grand canoe can stretch to nearly 40 feet in length, have a breadth of five feet, and weigh well over a ton. Hundreds of hands reach up to carry the great boat through the village, first, to the various builders' homes and, finally, with great singing and fanfare to the owner's home. There, the boat is lowered to the ground, and the owner and his crew climb aboard. Again the boat is raised overhead and borne to the beach.

On the beach the most sacred point of the boat launching ritual is reached. Quiet settles over the scene, and then the crew begins to chant. The boatmaster's wife — formally dressed, wearing a bead necklace and her traditional Yami field hat, and carrying a metal-tipped taro digging stick — steps to the water's edge. Her actions symbolize the waiting wife who anticipates her husband's successful return from the sea.

Men from all of the villages join in a ritual designed to repel demons and ghosts. They approach the canoe and gesticulate fiercely, fists raised and muscles bulging. They puff out their cheeks and grimace wildly, as they make aggressive gestures that their children imitate with great enthusiasm. Shamans offer prayers and incantations to ensure the boat will remain free of evil spirits.

After the cleansing frenzy the men raise the boat once again and ritually toss it into the air and catch it. This feat is performed three times. Then, at last, they carry it to the water and, for the first time, allow it to float in the ocean. The oars are affixed, the crew and master climb aboard, and the vessel is rowed rapidly out to sea to great cheering from those on the beach.

The launching officially ends the festival, but the splendid celebration will be remembered as a highlight for years to come. Launching a grand canoe is a major event, which takes place only occasionally, perhaps once every five years. In recent years, such launching festivals have attracted the attention of off-islanders. Tourists from Taiwan and Japan can now been seen at such events.

Chapter Nine

FESTIVAL
OF FLYING FISH

The Flying Fish Festival is an event rivaled in excitement and import only by the launching of a grand canoe. After all, the most important use of the Yami canoes is for fishing, in particular, taking in flying fish, which are a protein staple in the Yami diet. Flying fish, like many ocean fish, are migratory. For centuries they have moved along the Malay Gulf Stream to spawn in the cooler waters off the coast of Japan and the Aleutian Islands. Spring is when the flying fish run near Lan-yu.

As of this writing, the flying fish population in the Yami fishing grounds has suffered no major decline. However, that may not always be true. Industrialization along the Pacific Rim is causing pollution that, I was told by a Chinese ichthyologist, is threatening to change the migratory route of the flying fish. This problem is compounded by the use of dragnets by fishers from most countries in the area, including the People's Republic of China and Taiwan, Japan and Okinawa, Korea, Vietnam, and Malaysia. Five- or 10-mile-long dragnets ensnare the flying fish, which have no value to most of the fishers. The flying fish, which are killed by this method of fishing, are either thrown back into the ocean or harvested for use as animal food.

For now, but perhaps not forever, the Yami are unaffected by this problem.

Fishing from a boat in the open sea is far different from river or shoreline fishing, in which the Yami engage to a far lesser extent. Boat fishing requires strength and agility and, most of all, teamwork. The Yami crew, working together as if in one body, ensures not only a good catch but also a safe return from the often treacherous vastness of the Pacific.

The Yami fishing season begins in March and extends to late July or August. Yami men during this period devote their entire attention to fishing. But before they go to sea for the first expedition of the season, there is a festival during which the mystical aspects of fishing are exercised. It is not unusual for men to be lost at sea during the fishing season, and so this period is justifiably approached through ritual and faced with a mixture of excitement and foreboding.

In the days leading up to the Flying Fish Festival, the Yami men clean their boats, make repairs, and touch up the elaborately painted totems. Before they set out, the high bow and stern of each canoe also will be decorated with another type of totem. This object, constructed of wood and rooster feathers, is affixed to the high points of the boat and projects a little more than a foot above the bow and the stern.

The day of the Flying Fish Festival brings out the men and women in their finest attire. Men are again adorned in ceremonial armor, the most astonishing piece of which is the helmet that I described previously. This helmet is made of silver, which is said to have come to the island in the long-ago days when Portuguese traders roamed the Pacific. It has been suggested that the silver was obtained by melting down European coins, and the helmets most assuredly are among each family's most treasured possessions.

Yami women's dress includes a knee-length skirt of white and blue, roughly woven fabric, a simple blouse, and a vest, which usually also is blue and white. Beads, neck scarves, bracelets, and headbands complete the costume.

During the first part of the day, the men sit around, gossiping and smoking near the boats. The women, who do not go near the boats, cluster in the background. They bring cooking utensils, firewood, and fresh water to the festival site — along with pigs and chickens that later will be slaughtered.

At an appointed time in midafternoon the boatmasters of the large boats climb into their craft and walk to the bow. There, they are handed pigs and chickens, which they wave toward the sea. This gesture is to call the fish to come forth and be caught so that the Yami will have food for the next year.

The next phase of the festival ritual is the slaughtering of the pigs and chickens, whose blood is caught in cups. Young children from the village take the cups of blood and spread the blood at the edge of the beach where the ocean meets the shore. Fathers join their children in this activity and also smear blood on the boats. A small amount of blood is placed in containers that will be taken to sea, where the blood will be poured into the ocean near the fishing grounds. Commenting on the blood ritual 30 years ago, Father Hans Egli wrote:

> The simple and clear cry — "Come, come, come" — lets us imagine the magic ritual of the ice-age hunters. The offering of blood aims at protection for one's own life, safety in the boat, and an abundant catch of fish." (Egli 1968)

All of these activities are orchestrated by the senior boatmasters, who are the captains at sea. They are responsible for keeping their crews safe and ensuring a successful catch. And it is this cadre of boatmasters who determine when the ritual may be ended. The culmination of the festival is the feast itself. Everyone gathers on the beach for a meal of yams, water potatoes, and chicken. The village women cook and serve and listen to the men discuss their fishing strategies, but they have little to contribute to the conversation.

During the month that follows the Flying Fish Festival only the largest, 12-man canoes will go to sea. The explanation for this lies in the fact that the heaviest canoes are the safest during this period when heavy seas still prevail. As the season continues, however, the seas calm and smaller canoes put out. When putting to sea, the Yami men are orderly in their approach. They come to the beach with oars in hand, roll the canoes over the rocks or carry them overhead to the surf, and place the boats gently in the water. Water, which has been left in the boats to swell and tighten the planks, is baled.

The Yami men bring quantities of betel nuts (often referred to as Chinese chewing gum). These nuts are sucked or chewed. They contain about twice the caffeine of coffee and so serve as a mild stimulant. Red teeth and gums are telltales of the betel-nut chewer wherever one travels in Asia, but particularly in Chinese lands.

Another item that is brought into the boat is bundles of dried reeds. These bundles will be burned at sea, because they give off a bright light that attracts the flying fish.

Finally, the tension of the first day of fishing season bursts as the boats are pushed off. The crewmen jump aboard and take their oars. Rhythmically they stroke, faster and faster, singing to their efforts until the boats are pulled from sight of the village women, who watch their menfolk disappear in the vast expanse of the blue Pacific.

The trip to the fishing ground may take several hours, and they may be hours fraught with peril. The Yami canoes, while beautiful and fully seaworthy, are not built for rough seas. A sudden squall can spell disaster. But, with luck, the Yami fishermen reach their destination by midnight. Once there, they sit quietly until the darkest hour of the night (usually about 2 a.m.), for darkness is all-important for catching the elusive flying fish.

When the hour of deepest darkness arrives, a man near the front of the largest canoe sets alight one of the reed bundles and affixes it to the high point of the bow. The other men prepare nets that are attached to wooden hoops some four or five feet in diameter. (These nets now are woven from strong twine from China or Japan; in the past they were made from flax grown on Lan-yu.) Each net weighs about five pounds.

As the reed bundle burns brighter, the surrounding water comes alive with flying fish. These flying fish are a fascinating sight. The typical flying fish is 12 to 20 inches long and has elongated fins (the wings) that allow the fish to push itself powerfully from the water and to glide through the air for some distance at a height of two to 10 feet above the surface. "Flight" is primarily a defensive maneuver that allows the flying fish to escape from predators, such as sharks and aggressive species of fish. The bright light of the burning reeds draws them from the water by the hundreds, and the Yami net them in midair.

Once the netting begins, it may continue for several hours until the bottoms of the canoes are filled. Hundreds of fish will be caught before the boatmasters call a halt to the netting or the school of flying fish moves off. Only then will the canoes be turned homeward or, if more fish are needed, toward another fishing ground.

During the next phase, whether homeward or toward a new location, some of the men will set out lines. These lines are baited with small, bleeding flying fish and dragged through the water as the boat is rowed along. The fish blood attracts larger predators. I have seen a 50-pound fish caught in this way. But occasionally the dragline will be struck by something really large, such as a shark, and a man may be literally ripped from the canoe. (I should point out that any large fish caught in this manner is destined for consumption by men only; women are entitled only to smaller fish.)

As dawn breaks, the fishermen pull for home. When they finally return to Lan-yu, they pull the canoes ashore and begin to unload their catch. The fish are carried into the village to the porches of the fishermen's houses. There, they are scaled, gutted, and rubbed with salt. The salt, incidentally, is gathered from dry salt beds that can be found scattered around the island or, more-so in recent times, purchased at markets in Taiwan. Twine is used to gather bundles of three to six fish apiece, and the bundles are hung from poles to dry in the hot sun. The catch will be shared equitably among the family and with others who may be owed a share of the catch in exchange for some service.

After their long ordeal at sea, once the canoes have been stowed and the catch cared for, the men wash and eat a breakfast of yams and dried fish. Then they retire to the shady decks of their summer houses to talk, smoke, and sleep away the day.

Canoes, both large and small, wait on the shore.

Although meat does not play a central role in the Yami diet, pork is universally served during festivals. Before they become part of a feast, pigs serve as natural "garbage disposals" for the busy Yami households.

Flying fish, seen in this photograph hanging in bundles to dry, are a staple of the Yami diet. Their odor permeates the villages.

In Chapter Seven I briefly described the Yami meals and general diet. This is perhaps as good a place as any to go into a bit more detail — beginning with the flying fish. Flying fish are eaten year-round, and the most recent catch will not be touched until the existing supply has been exhausted. This practice ensures freshness during the nonfishing months.

What does flying fish taste like? Perhaps the best comparison is country ham with a strong flavor of fish and a texture similar to beef jerky. The odor of dried flying fish also is strong and permeates every village. Every Yami carries the pungent scent on hands and breath. (During my visits to Lan-yu, Yami friends presented me with gifts of flying fish, which I did not refuse out of politeness but could not keep and took pains to discard without offending my generous hosts.)

I mentioned previously that the Yami do not follow the dietary regimen of the Chinese. Tea, wine, soft drinks, noodles, stewed fish, steamed bread, and other staples of Chinese cuisine are eschewed. And they have a particular dislike of rice. Indeed, various influences from beyond the island to expand the Yami diet have been consistently rejected. Instead, the Yami eat dried flying fish, taro root, yams, millet, and water potatoes.

As I mentioned previously, the Yami eat two meals each day. These meals consist of the same foods, though breakfast is a somewhat lighter meal than dinner. A mealtime staple is soup flavored with flying fish and tubers. Meat often is cooked in large pots of salted water. And the meat broth is served in a soup bowl and called *waga*.

The meats in the Yami diet are consumed less often but include goat, pig, chicken, and occasionally wild birds (which are barbecued on a stick over hot coals). Meats are always included on festival occasions but eaten only occasionally during other times. Pork is probably the most popular meat, and piglets are castrated soon after birth to ensure that their meat will be sweet.

During a visit to Lan-yu in 1997, I had the opportunity to watch a Yami family prepare a pork dinner. A pig was killed by slitting its throat. Its entrails were removed, and the body hair was burnt and scraped off. The carcass was then cut into several pieces, which were thoroughly washed in salt water. Then the meat was placed over hot coals and covered with coals and banana leaves, which had the effect of both broiling and steaming the flesh. I must confess that fear of trichinosis prevented me from sampling this dish, as the Yami eat their pork rare.

The pork in the Yami diet has a side benefit: Pigpens function as ecologically sound garbage disposals, because the pigs eat all of the Yami leftovers. Chickens provide another side benefit as a source of feathers, which the Yami use to decorate their canoes; and chicken blood also is used on ceremonial occasions. As a rule the Yami do not eat chicken eggs; instead, they feed them to their pigs.

The islanders also enjoy several varieties of fish in addition to flying fish. These other fish may be caught by anglers on the shore or by net-casters who stand waist-deep in the ocean shallows. The Yami catch freshwater shrimp in mountain streams and use them for bait. Some Yami men also are talented in spear fishing and diving for clams and lobsters.

But most of the Yami's food is cultivated: foxtail millet, asparagus beans, hyacinth beans, yams, and so on. Fruit is in short supply, particularly citrus varieties, which means that the Yami diet lacks vitamin C. The fruits available consist mainly of plums, hybrid bananas, and coconuts. Ginger and wild sugar cane also can be found on the island.

The Yami use wet-field cultivation for moisture-dependent crops, such as taro root and yams, a cultivation technique known to Taiwan only since the 15th century. (The Yami prefer to cultivate the wet-field taro root, rather than the dry-field taro root more popular with aboriginal groups on Taiwan.) They bring the water to the fields in buckets or by constructing ditches and canals. The manner of irrigation often depends on the lay of the land, for on Lan-yu level land is scarce. Most fields are terraced.

Finally, though not a food stuff, the betel nut bears mention. As many readers know, betel nuts are popular in many parts of Asia, and the Yami are especially fond of this stimulant. Tobacco, however, is even more popular; but it is not grown on Lan-yu. Gifts of cigarettes from visitors are especially welcomed.

Chapter
Ten

NEW SCHOOLS, NEW IDEAS

Education shapes — and reshapes — culture, as much as it is shaped by culture. Thus politics and pedagogy often go hand in hand. Educating the young on Lan-yu is no longer simply the prerogative of parents, clans, and the Yami people in general. Formal education under the auspices of the Taiwan Ministry of Education and the regional Department of Education has now arrived.

Official policy requires children to begin formal schooling at the age of six or seven. Chinese elementary schools are found in each village, and Yami children wear school uniforms that are typical of school children in China and Japan. No tuition is charged, and classes tend to be small, perhaps five to seven pupils with a teacher. Textbooks and other supplies, including the school uniforms, are provided by the Taiwan government.

The subjects taught also are typical of Chinese schools found on Taiwan. Chinese, history, mathematics, physical education, science, and social studies dominate the curriculum. The Yami resent the imposition of formal schools and, in particular, the emphasis on Chinese language instruction, because they view Chinese as an imposed foreign language. But such resentment is slowly weakening.

Because school schedules do not accommodate traditional activities, Chinese officials have found regular attendance to be a nearly unreachable goal. Parents need their children at home to babysit younger siblings and to help with chores. Attendance is highest during the winter months. But when fishing season begins in March, the numbers fall off. During late spring, when girls are expected to help with farming and husbandry chores, attendance dives even lower. Overall school attendance during grades one through six averages about 60%.

After children complete the sixth grade, they may go on to junior high school. However, few Yami children take this step, even though an excellent junior high school can now be found on Lan-yu. The children who attend this school board there and then return to their homes on weekends. The school spans grades seven through nine. The evidence that resistance to formal education is weakening can be seen in the growth of this school's population. The number of students attending junior high school grew from only 30 students in 1970 to more than 250 by 1992.

An even smaller number of Yami youth pursue formal schooling beyond grade nine. There is no high school on Lan-yu as yet. The few young people who do go on to high school must enter a competitive high school on Taiwan, which is a major step. Not only is the prospect of more advanced schooling daunting, but also it requires the nearly unthinkable: leaving the island.

Most ninth-grade graduates, like their sixth-grade counterparts, go to work in their native villages. I should mention as well that in 1994 the Chinese government instituted a military service requirement for all of the aboriginal peoples of Taiwan. All boys at some point must face this requirement.

The logic of the Chinese government is straightforward. By bringing the Yami into Chinese society — through schooling, military service, and the like — it is hoped that the Yami will be strengthened as a people — *if* they are willing to meld their old ways with the ways of modern Chinese society. Making the Yami part of the "Chinese family," termed *Sinofication*, is seen by the government on Taiwan as a way to prevent the island from becoming a reservation with the Yami as wards of the state.

As might be imagined, the Yami view is quite different. The Yami see themselves as an independent and self-sufficient people, a proud people with distinct traditions and a unique culture. Their island, for them, is a nation-state; and the Chinese (and others) are interlopers. Yet the Yami attitudes are changing. They like some of the benefits that they derive from Chinese attention. And so, though the Yami have not become Sinophiles, they are becoming less and less Sinophobic as the years pass. Education is part of the reason for this transition.

And so, let me say a bit more about educational matters.

A few years ago professors from Taiwan attempted to study the intellectual level of the Yami people. They administered IQ tests to Yami first-graders and found that the youngsters were similar to their age mates on Taiwan. When they repeated this procedure with ninth-graders, however, the results were not similar. Yami youngsters evidenced markedly lower IQs, compared to their age mates on Taiwan. The Yami ninth-graders were particularly deficient in math and science.

The conclusion of the psychometricians pointed mainly to environmental factors as reasons for the discrepancy. The Yami use little in the way of money or measurement that is comparable to modern society, thus the students had little exposure to the day-to-day mathematics on which abstract math concepts are built. The same could be said of science. The limitations of island living were evident in a lack of exposure to larger concepts, and both of those types of limitation translated into lower IQ scores.

By contrast, the Yami are seen as advanced in such areas as language, music, and art — areas not measured by IQ tests — for which their cultural traditions might be said to be instrumental. To take a more recent view, I suspect that in terms of multiple intelligences (à la Howard Gardner) the Yami are on par with their Taiwan age mates in every sense, a fact that has largely escaped traditional measures of "intelligence."

Interestingly, on my first trip to Lan-yu I met two Yami individuals who had completed college. They told me that a total of six Yami had taken college degrees, most in education or military science. When these individuals finished college, they returned to the island as government employees and worked in Lan-yu's small bureaucratic center. Needless to say, these individuals were the pride of the Chinese; but, surprisingly, they also were the pride of the Yami.

The Chinese see the education of the Yami as a major goal, something that was never the case during the 50-year Japanese occupation. The Japanese mission did not choose to assist the Yami to change from their preliterate state; but the Chinese are quite dogged in pursuit of this end. It must be said, however, that even as Chinese formal education is making inroads, traditional Yami education continues. Fathers teach their sons; mothers teach their daughters. All work side-by-side in the fields and workshops. And few children — albeit a growing number — are drawn to life outside the traditions. Indeed, to a great extent, children are miniature adults. Boys, once past the nudity of childhood, dress as their fathers do; girls as their mothers dress. Their toys are small-scale replicas of adult boats, fishing equipment, farm tools, and cooking utensils — the staples of island life.

Boys and girls observe and act out the rituals in which their parents take part. Yami boys take great pleasure in inflating their cheeks and chasing ghosts. They delight in launching small canoes and learning the basics of fishing in the shallows near the beaches. Girls mimic the dances of their mothers and older sisters. Moreover, there are no special rites of passage. The transitions from childhood to adolescence, from adolescence to adulthood, are relatively seamless in the Yami culture.

These are aspects of Yami culture that the Yami themselves see as essential to preserve. Will they be able to do so? That is a hard question to answer, but the prospects do not seem altogether bright. Formal school — the mix of pedagogy and politics — increasingly is consuming the time during childhood that once was the exclusive province of the Yami cultural traditions. And time, even in the seemingly timeless idyll of Lan-yu, is a factor. As more and more time is devoted to learning Chinese, acquiring school skills, practicing calligraphy, and so on, less and less time is left to learn boat building, farming, fishing, and dancing. Can Sinofication occur and still leave time for the maintenance of tradition, the sustenance of culture? Time, as they say, will tell.

Chapter
Eleven

THE LEƧƧON
OF LAN-YU

In 1895 the Japanese occupied Taiwan and the surrounding islands, including Lan-yu. In the modern era they were the least disruptive to island life of Lan-yu's overlords. Even today the Yami retain a certain fondness for the Japanese, because they intruded so little on their traditional culture.

Near the end of the Japanese occupation in 1945, the colonial administration did set up schools to teach Japanese and to encourage Yami loyalty to the emperor of Japan. Police and military personnel were billeted on the island. But, on the whole, the Japanese treated Lan-yu specifically as a living anthropological museum. They limited the number of visitors to the island and thus the outside influences on the Yami culture. If they can be faulted in any particular area, I suggest that it may be simply that they introduced tobacco to the island; and the Yami took it up with relish. Cigarettes today are evident everywhere on the island and are used as gifts and in bartering.

But the period of Japanese occupation was an interlude. The main, albeit intermittent, influence competing with Yami traditions is Chinese culture. The Chinese have governed Lan-yu in one way or another apparently since time immemorial. Chinese archeologists have found items on the island that date from the Sung Dynasty, evidence that suggests Chinese interest in — and an outpost on — Lan-yu since at least the 9th century.

77

It is the persistence and pervasiveness of Chinese culture that is intruding on and, I fear, supplanting traditional Yami culture. The Yami are keenly aware of this but also as keenly aware that they hold no power to resist the advance of "civilization."

The romantic in me sees a pristine paradise in peril. What is this "civilization" that will replace the gentle society and colorful traditions of the Yami people, who are as "civilized" in their own way as any people on earth? And why? I suggested in the previous chapter that the Chinese desire not to rid the Yami of their traditions but, instead, to empower them *in addition* to cope with the modern world that increasingly intrudes on their solitude in the vast Pacific. And yet, in the process of this empowerment, something is to be lost. The "splendid isolation" of the Yami's island cannot resist the inroads made by advances in transportation and communication — inroads not only physical but also psychological and emotional. Television alone will forever change the Yami, not to mention the increasing number of visitors each year.

The Yami are a gentle people. Harmony with their environment and with their neighbors is a close-held value. The fighting that has marred Chinese relations with other island cultures has not touched Lan-yu, where the Yami have avoided conflict and bloodshed. Can this peace-loving people resist the "peaceful" invasion of the modern world, of Chinese education, of television? At heart, I know they cannot.

On the other hand, the pragmatist in me recognizes that Lan-yu, for all its natural beauty and the gentleness of its inhabitants, is far from idyllic in other ways. Infanticide, illness, lack of proper nutrition, and short life spans all may be combated through education, health care, and the influx of modern ideas, influences, and products — all of which seem to be inevitable in any case.

Isolation anywhere on earth, I suspect, is no longer possible. Certainly that can be said of Lan-yu. Not too many years ago, it was rare for a non-Yami to be permitted to stay on the island overnight. Now there is a hotel and a restaurant for visitors. The natural lagoon on the east side of the island has been enhanced as a harbor to better permit tourist and supply boats to dock. A hospital, an airport, and, as I mentioned earlier in this book, a "civilized" road around the circumference of the island — all are changing life on Lan-yu.

Elementary schools exist in every village. An increasing number of students attends the single junior high school. Perhaps a high school is not far in the future, and doubtless more young people each year will choose to attend school for a longer time. Obligatory military service for Yami men introduces new points of view, as do the personalities they hear and see on radio and television. Although most youngsters still shed their school uniforms and run naked on the beach, can "civilized" clothing for casual attire be too far off? Money has been introduced; and where currency is available, commerce follows.

While the metaphor of an anthropological museum or zoo is elitist, even demeaning to the Yami, there is something to be said for pausing to consider the Yami of Lan-yu for their traditional culture. Rousseau's notion of the "noble savage" may be out of fashion, but we can nonetheless benefit from examining the Yami way of life, the harmony in which they coexist with their island world, and even the way they allow outside influences gradually to reshape their culture. The Yami can show us values that often seem to get left behind in the rush to "civilization," such as the values of sharing, of community, of childhood innocence and adult modesty.

I have prized my time on Lan-yu among the Yami for these reasons — not because they are "primitive" in a "civilized" world, but because they display a civilization, internally in conflict, both intact and in transition, that contrasts with my own. I fear that my grandchildren may not live in a world in which such contrasts are allowed to exist, a world in which peoples like the Yami have been subsumed, absorbed, mutated into — ourselves. I learn from the Yami. In them I see a distinct culture with rich traditions. But, equally, I learn from them about my own culture. And, perhaps as important, I learn about cultural transition and the inevitability of change.

The German writer Herman Hesse wrote, "He who travels far will often see things far from what he believed was truth." The

Yami show us another truth, another civilization. In viewing that truth, we may better discern the truths of our own culture. That, I believe, is the real lesson of Lan-yu.

RESOURCES

A number of books proved to be valuable in my quest for understanding about the Yami and Lan-yu. It appears that the best studies may be those published in Japanese, a language that I do not know. Thus I relied on works in English and Chinese.

Benedict, Ruth. *Patterns of Culture.* Boston: Houghton Mifflin, 1934.

Birdsell, J.B. "The Problem of Early Peopling of the Americas as Viewed from Asia." In *Papers in Physical Anthropogy*, edited by W.S. Laughlin. New York: Viking Fund, 1949.

Boas, Franz. *The Mind of Primitive Man.* New York: Macmillan, 1911.

Burkert, Walter. *Creation of the Sacred: Tracks of Biology in Early Religions.* Cambridge, Mass.: Harvard University Press, 1997.

Chen, Chi-Lu. *Material Culture of the Formosan Aborigines.* Taipei: Taiwan Museum, 1988.

Davis, Charles M. *South Sea Islands.* Garden City, N.Y.: Doubleday, 1957.

Dixon, R.B. *The Racial History of Man.* New York: Charles Scribner's Sons, 1923.

Dixon, R.B. *The Building of Cultures.* New York: Charles Scribner's Sons, 1928.

Egli, Hans, S.J. *Yami.* Taipei: Catholic Church of Taiwan, 1968.

Formosan Aboriginal Culture Village: A Yami Introduction. Booklet in Chinese. Taipei: Nantou Press of Taiwan, 1997.

Freeman, Otis W., ed. *Geography of the Pacific.* New York: John Wiley and Sons, 1951.

Goddard, W.G. *Formosa: A Study in Chinese History.* New York, Macmillan, 1966.

Heyerdahl, Thor. *American Indians in the Pacific.* London: George Allen and Unwin, 1952.

Heyerdahl, Thor. "Feasible Ocean Routes to and from the Americas in Pre-Columbian Times." *American Antiquity* 28 (1963): 482-88.

Jeng Huey-Ing, "The Yami Boat Culture." *Bulletin of Ethnology*, Academia Sinica (1984): 33-81. (Chinese)

Kano, Tadao. "Lan-yu: Boat Building Ceremony." *Human Culture Magazine* (1938). (Japanese)

Kano, Tadao. "South Asian Boat Building." *Southeast Asian Journal* (1946). (Japanese)

Kano, Tadao, and Segawa, Kokichi. *An Illustrated Ethnography of Formosan Aborigines.* vol. 1. Tokyo: Maruzen, 1956.

Li, Dun J. *The Ageless Chinese.* New York: Charles Scribner's Sons, 1978.

Mackay, George Leslie: *From Far Formosa.* New York: Fleming H. Revell, 1895.

Newman, M.T. "The Application of Ecological Rules to the Racial Anthropology of the Aboriginal New World." *American Anthropologist* 55 (1953): 311-27.

Peng, Yunghai. *Customs and Traditions in Plain and Highlands of Taiwan.* Taipei: Cave Press, 1972.

Reid, Daniel P. *Taiwan.* Hong Kong: APA Productions (HK), 1984.

Reid, Daniel P. *Images of Taiwan.* Hong Kong: Hong Kong Publishing Company, 1984.

Shye Ing Jhou. *Beauty of Lan-yu.* Taipei: Chinese Cultural University, 1984. (Chinese)

Sih, Paul K.T., ed. *Taiwan in Modern Times.* New York: St. John's University Press, 1973.

Simmons, R.T. "A Report on Blood Group Genetical Surveys in Eastern Asia, Indonesia, Melanesia, Micronesia, Polynesia, and Australia in the Study of Man." *Anthropos* 51 (1956): 500-12.

Smith, Douglas C. "The Chinese Family in Transition: An Occidental Interpretation of Taiwan." *Asian Culture Quarterly* 20 (Fall 1992): 40-75.

Smith, Douglas C. "The Confucius-Dewey Synthesis: A Comparative Analysis of the Philosophic and Pedagogic Ideas of Kung Fu-tze and John Dewey." *Asian Culture Quarterly* 24 (Fall 1996): 1-27.

Smith, Douglas C. "Theoretical Dimensions of Chinese Education Philosophy and Thought." *Asian Culture Quarterly* 18 (Spring 1990): 1-16.

Strathern, Marilyn. "Cultural Diversity." *Bulletin of Ethnology*, Academia Sinica, No. 78, Taiwan, 1994.

Swindler, David R. *A Racial Study of the West Nakanai.* Philadelphia: University of Pennsylvania Press, 1962.

Takekoshi, Yasoburo. *Japanese Rule in Formosa.* London: Longmans, Green, and Company, 1907, 1978.

Thomas, William L. "The Pacific Basin." In *Peoples and Cultures of the Pacific*, edited by A.P. Vayda. New York: Natural History Press, 1968.

Toates, Frederick. *Biological Foundations of Behavior.* London: Open University Press, 1986.

"View of Lan-yu" (Taipei) *Bright China: Chinese-English Bilingual Monthly* (December 1986): 5-9.

Wichard, Claude R., ed. "Climate and Man." U.S. Department of Agriculture booklet. Washington, D.C., 1941.

Wu Che-gung. *In Touch with Lan-yu.* Taipei: Taipei Press, 1986. (Chinese).

ABOUT THE AUTHOR

Douglas C. Smith is a professor and director of the West Virginia University Graduate Center. Smith holds six earned university degrees, including a Ph.D. in history from West Virginia University (1975). In 1993, he also was awarded an honorary Litt.D. for his writing, research, and teaching in the field of comparative education. Since 1977, he has been senior visiting professor of history and languages at a number of Asian universities.

Smith is a Fellow of the Korea Foundation, the Pacific Cultural Foundation of Taiwan, and formerly, Visiting Fellow at Teachers College Columbia University. He is the author of five books, including *Elementary Teacher Education in Korea* (1994), the first volume in the International Studies in Education series published by the Phi Delta Kappa Educational Foundation. He also is the author of numerous articles on comparative education, history, and Asian family life. Smith is a frequent visitor to Asia and currently is working on a project that looks at the impact of westernization and modernization on the traditional Confucian relational system.

DATE DUE

GAYLORD			PRINTED IN U.S.A.